WHEN GOD
LEFT FOOTPRINTS

D1457367

PAM & STAN CAMPBELL

WHEN GOD LEFT FOOTPRINTS

VICTOR BOOKS®

A DIVISION OF SCRIPTURE PRESS PUBLICATIONS INC.
USA CANADA ENGLAND

BibleLog Thru the New Testament Series
Book 1 **When God Left Footprints** (Matthew thru John)
Book 2 **Good News to Go** (Acts thru 1 Corinthians)
Book 3 **Priority Mail** (2 Corinthians thru Philemon)
Book 4 **Home At Last** (Hebrews thru Revelation)

BibleLog Thru the Old Testament Series
Book 1 **Let There Be Life** (Genesis thru Ruth)
Book 2 **Who's Running This Kingdom?** (1 Samuel thru 2 Chronicles)
Book 3 **Tales, Tunes, and Truths** (Ezra thru Song of Songs)
Book 4 **Watchmen Who Wouldn't Quit** (Isaiah thru Malachi)

BibleLog for Adults is an inductive Bible study series designed to take you through the Bible in 2 years if you study one session each week. This eight-book series correlates with SonPower's **BibleLog** series for youth. You may want to use **BibleLog** in your daily quiet time, completing a chapter a week by working through a few pages each day. Or you may want to use this series (along with the SonPower **BibleLog** series) in family devotions with your teenagers. This book also includes a leader's guide for use in small groups.

Scripture taken from the *Holy Bible, New International Version,* © 1973, 1978, 1984, International Bible Society. Used by permission of Zondervan Bible Publishers.

Library of Congress Catalog Card Number: 91-65462
ISBN: 0-89693-867-0

Recommended Dewey Decimal Classification: 226.1
Suggested Subject Heading: BIBLE STUDY: GOSPELS

C O N T E N T S

BEFORE YOU BEGIN

Welcome to Book 1 in the
BibleLog Thru the New Testament Series

Though the Bible continues to be one of the world's best-selling books, few people are familiar enough with it to comprehend "the big picture." They may know many of the specific stories about Abraham, Samson, Jonah, Jesus, Peter, Paul, and so forth. Yet most people are unsure how these characters fit into the broad historic groupings—patriarchs, judges, kings, prophets, Gospels, epistles, etc.

That's why we are introducing the **BibleLog Thru the New Testament Series.** The purpose of the **BibleLog** studies is to guide you through the New Testament in one year, at the rate of one session per week. This series eliminates the perceived drudgery of Bible reading by removing unnecessary references and explaining the material in clear terms that anyone can understand. The pace should be fast enough to propel you through the material without getting bogged down, yet slow enough to allow you to see things you never noticed before. First-time readers will feel completely at ease as they explore the Bible on their own. Yet no matter how many times a person has been through the Bible, this study will provide fresh insight.

WHAT MAKES BIBLELOG DIFFERENT?
Countless thousands of adults have, at some point in their lives, decided to read through the Bible. Pastors, Sunday School teachers, Bible study leaders, or peers have preached the benefits of "Read your Bible," "Get into the Word," "Meditate on Scripture," and so forth. And after hearing so many worthwhile challenges, a lot of determined, committed adults have dusted off the covers of their Bibles and set themselves to the task ahead.

They usually make a noble effort too. The first couple of Bible books whiz past before they know it. The next few books aren't quite as fast-paced, but they have their strong points. Then comes a tough passage. In most cases, the Gospels are enough to do in even the most eager readers. And instead of feeling like they've accomplished something, all that those people feel is guilt because they didn't finish what they started.

That's why this Bible study series was developed. It calls for a one-year commitment on your part to get through the New Testament. By following the session plans provided, you only need to complete one session each week to accomplish your one-year goal. You won't read the entire New Testament word-for-word, but you will go much more in-depth than most of the New Testament overviews you may have tried. You will still be challenged just to get through the major flow of New Testament action in one year.

WHAT ARE THE FEATURES OF BIBLELOG?

❑ **THE WHOLE BIBLE** Not a verse-by-verse study, but an approach that hits all the books without skipping major passages.

❑ **THE RIGHT PACE** By completing one session each week (a couple of pages per day), you will get through the New Testament in one year.

❑ **A FRESH APPROACH** The inductive design allows you to personally interact with biblical truth. Longer, drier passages are summarized in the text, and difficult passages are explained, but you are kept involved in the discovery process at all times.

❑ **INSTANT APPLICATION** Each weekly session concludes with a **Journey Inward** section of practical application that allows you to respond to the content immediately. The goal is to help you apply the truths of the Bible today.

❑ **GROUP STUDY OPTION** A leader's guide is included to promote discussion and further application, if desired. After a week of self-study, a time of group interaction can be very effective in reinforcing God's truth. Each book covers 13 weeks.

❑ **REASONABLE PRICE** The entire set of 4 New Testament BibleLog books costs no more than a basic Bible commentary. And after completing the series, you will have a self-written commentary of the New Testament for future reference.

❑ **48 DIFFERENT TOPICS** Over a one-year period of study, you will be challenged to apply what the Bible has to say about 48 different topics, including your relationship with Jesus, rejection, integrity, commitment, self-image, empathy, eternity, and much more.

HOW CAN YOU GET THE MOST OUT OF BIBLELOG?

We recommend a group study for this series, if possible. If group members work through the content of the sessions individually during the week, the time your group needs to spend going over facts will be greatly reduced. With the content portion completed prior to the group meeting, your group time can emphasize the application of the biblical concepts to your individual members. A leader's guide is included at the back of the book to direct you in a review of the content. But the real strength of the leader's guide is to show you how to apply what you are learning. If you don't have the opportunity to go through this series with a group, that's OK too. Just be sure to think through all the **Journey Inward** sections at the end of each session.

FROM THE AUTHORS

This book is titled *When God Left Footprints* and its approach is a little different from the other books in the **BibleLog** series. It will focus on the Gospels—Matthew, Mark, Luke, and John. But unlike the other **BibleLog** studies, this one won't go through one Bible book at a time. Since each of these four writers provided a biography of the life of Jesus, we will try to synthesize what they had to say to get as complete a picture of the life of Jesus as possible. So get ready to do some bouncing back and forth through these four Gospels.

As you study Matthew, Mark, Luke, and John, try to discover as much as you can about the Son of God. The hard-to-comprehend truth about Him is that while He was 100 percent God, when He walked on earth He was also 100 percent human. He was God in human form, or the God who left footprints. You will see that early in His ministry, Jesus didn't want the word to spread too quickly about who He was. But you will also discover that He later made it very clear that He was indeed God.

If you want to know more about what God is like, follow His footsteps through the Gospels. And if you want to become more like Jesus, invite Him to take a closer look at you. As you discover more of what Jesus is like and open up to Him, you can develop a genuine relationship with God. Make it your goal as you journey through this book to get closer to God every week.

Pam & Stan Campbell

Do we ever overlook valuable objects
because they don't appear to be valuable?

IT'S BEGINNING TO LOOK A LOT LIKE CHRISTMAS

(Jesus' Birth)

In 1986 a man went to a mineral show in Arizona. Before he left home, his two sons each gave him $5 and asked him to pick a pretty polished stone as a souvenir. As the man walked through one of the rock shops, he spotted a particular stone priced at $15. But since the stone didn't look as pretty as most of the others, the owner let the man purchase it for $10.

The man had just made a good deal—much better than the owner ever expected. The stone was the world's largest star sapphire, weighing in at 1,905 carats and estimated at around $2.5 million. After the news of the big sale broke, how would you like to have been one of the people who had recently been to the mineral show? Would you have passed over the stone, perhaps thinking that $15 was a ridiculously high price to ask for one crummy little rock?

Stories abound of similar instances. A painting hangs in an obscure gallery for years, until one day an art expert happens to see it and identifies it as an undiscovered (and priceless) Renoir, Matisse, O'Keefe, or Piccaso. Old pieces of furniture sit in a barn, worthless to their owners and forgotten for years until they are carted away by the junkman, bought by a knowledgeable refinisher, and restored as valuable antiques. And you don't need an eye for star sapphires to find some terrific rocks in the right creek beds. What looks like dull, round, brown stones to some people are actually geodes that are eagerly scooped up by others. When broken open, their hollow centers are surrounded by brilliant crystals of quartz or other minerals.

The world is full of valuable artifacts that, because they don't appear to be valuable, are overlooked by many, many people. But to people who are able to identify them, those same artifacts bring great joy and satisfaction.

 JOURNEY ONWARD

In the Old Testament, the prophets were very specific in predicting the coming of the Messiah. They had prepared the people for the coming of a "Wonderful Counselor, Mighty God, Everlasting Father, Prince of Peace" (Isaiah 9:6). And the Jewish people were ready for a king to come riding in to save the day for them.

In the approximately 400 years between the end of the Old Testament and the beginning of the New Testament, the people of God had seen a lot of changes. The Babylonians had originally conquered them, but then the Babylonians were defeated by the Persians. The Persians were in turn defeated by the Greeks (under Alexander the Great), who did much to spread the Greek language and culture throughout the known world. During most of this time, Israel (who had become only a minor territory among the megapowers of the world) was allowed to maintain its religious practices.

But after the death of Alexander the Great, his successors weren't so tolerant of the Jews. A man came to power in 175 B.C. named Antiochus (IV) Epiphanes, who wanted to eliminate the Jews. He tried to destroy all their religious writings and he forbade many of their worship ceremonies. But the biggest insult he inflicted on the Jewish people was offering a pig (an "unclean" animal) to a statue of Zeus he had set up in their temple in Jerusalem.

Before long, some of the Jews (including Judas Maccabeus and his brothers) had organized a revolt. The Israelites fought this "Maccabean revolt" from 166–142 B.C., and finally won their independence until the Romans came to power in 63 B.C. The Romans besieged Jerusalem for three months, and when they finally entered the city they killed many of the priests and entered the most holy place in the temple.

With the Romans in control and the Israelites resentful, the people were looking for God's promised Messiah who would deliver them from their oppressors and give them peace. And God sent that Messiah, but He came in a "plain brown wrapper," so to speak.

Skim Matthew 1:1-17; Luke 3:23-38.

First we need to look at Jesus' genealogy. Both Matthew and Luke provide a family tree for us to examine. Which of Jesus' ancestors are you are familiar with? *Abraham, Isaac, Jacob, Judah, Boaz + Ruth, Jesse, David Solomon, → Joseph / Shem, Noah, Methuselah, Seth, Adam, God*

Notice that the writers are careful not to say that Joseph was Jesus' real father (Matthew 1:16; Luke 3:23). Sometimes Joseph and Mary are referred to as husband and wife, even before Jesus was born. Like our culture today, couples were formally engaged for a period of time before the actual wedding. But unlike our culture, the engagements of that time were legally binding. If the couple wanted to break their engagement, they had to get a divorce. And while the engagement was almost the same as the real wedding from a legal standpoint, there was clearly to be no sexual activity until the wedding itself. We meet Mary and Joseph at the point in their relationship after the engagement, but before the wedding.

Special Deliveries
Read Luke 1:5-20, 57-66.
But the Christmas story doesn't really begin with Mary and Joseph. What couple was first concerned with having a baby? (Luke 1:5-7)
Zechariah + Elizabeth

What news did God send this man? How did he respond to the news? (Luke 1:8-18) *God sent the message that Zechariah's wife, who was older + barren, would have a child. Zechariah asked how he would know it would really happen.*

What happened to him because of his response? (Luke 1:19-20) *Zechariah could not speak until the baby had actually been born.*

Gabriel's message came true right away. Elizabeth, in spite of her advanced age, became pregnant. Zechariah (or "Zacharias," depending on your Bible translation) was a proud father, and he gave God credit for all that had happened. When the time came for Elizabeth to have her baby, how did Zechariah show that he wanted to do as Gabriel had instructed? (Luke 1:57-63) *They named him John as the angel had foretold.*

What happened as Zechariah proved his faithfulness to God? (Luke 1:64-66) *He was again able to speak.*

Read Matthew 1:18-25.
A lot of angelic activity was taking place during this time. Joseph was also visited by an angel. What kind of person do you think Joseph was? (Matthew 1:18-19) *Quiet, sympathetic, kind*

What instructions did the angel give to Joseph? (Matthew 1:20-25)
take Mary as his wife + name the child Jesus

Read Luke 1:1–2:38.
The name "Jesus" means "the Lord saves." And God made it clear that He was the one responsible for sending Jesus. In addition to Joseph and Zechariah, Mary received an angelic visitor. What news did the angel deliver? (Luke 1:26-33) *That Mary was favored, that she would bear a child conceived by the Holy Spirit + that child would be the Son of God.*

Why did Mary have a problem understanding what Gabriel told her? (Luke 1:34) How did she respond after Gabriel explained the situation to her? (Luke 1:35-38) *She was a virgin. She said she was the Lord's servant + accepted what would happen.*

Mary was related to Elizabeth, so she went to Elizabeth's house for a three-month visit while both of them were pregnant (Luke 1:56). Notice what happened as the two expectant mothers got together (Luke 1:39-45).
Elizabeth's child (John) leaped in the womb.
Joseph lived in Nazareth, a city in Galilee. But according to the Prophet Micah, the Messiah was to be born in Bethlehem (Micah 5:2). So how was it that Jesus was born in Bethlehem instead of Nazareth? (Luke 2:1-7)
Joseph to Mary to be registered in Bethlehem which was the home of his ancestors. This was decreed by Emperor Augustus

You've probably heard this story so many times that the feelings might be getting lost in the facts. Try to imagine what Mary and Joseph must have been thinking and feeling. Mary was probably a young woman. She was expecting a baby, even though she had never had sexual intercourse. She wasn't even married to the man she was with. She was away from home, with its comforts and familiar surroundings. After a three-day journey, she and Joseph couldn't even get a room for the night. And after all this, she had her baby while staying overnight in some place other than the inn. (Notice that the Bible never says that Jesus was born in a stable. The manger is the only clue we have to go on, and the manger could just as easily have been in a cave.)

Getting Personal—*Put yourself in Mary's or Joseph's place. How would you have responded in the same situation? What kinds of questions would you have had for the angel?*

Why do you think God allowed His Son to be born under such conditions?

to show his humility, to show that he was a regular man (not obviously of royal birth)

Even though Jesus wasn't exactly given a royal welcome with kingly attendants, festive celebrations, or baby showers, God didn't allow His birth to go completely unnoticed. Who were the first people to help celebrate Jesus' birth, and how did they find out what was going on? (Luke 2:8-20)

Shepherds — from the angels

There were a couple of other people who saw the Baby Jesus who aren't always remembered at Christmas. Like any other Jewish boy, Jesus was circumcised when He was eight days old (Luke 2:21). And at the temple were two people who recognized that this baby was definitely someone special. Who were the two people and what did they reveal about Jesus? (Luke 2:25-38)

Simeon + Anna both knew he was the messiah

Read Matthew 2:1-23.

Another group of people wanted to honor Jesus, but they had a problem. Who were these people, and what did they need to know? (Matthew 2:1-8) To whom did they go for help? What help and instructions did they receive?

The wise men. They needed directions + went to Herod. they rec'd directions to Bethlehem + instructions to return + tell Herod. they didn't return.

15

When they finally found Jesus, how did they honor Him? (Matthew 2:9-11)

gifts of gold, frankincense & myrrh

Notice a few things about this group of people. Nowhere does the Bible say that these men were kings, or that there were three of them. (There were three gifts, but the number of people was never specifically stated.) Also notice that when these people finally found Jesus, He and His parents were in a house (Matthew 2:11). So the Nativity scenes that portray Mary, Joseph, Jesus, the shepherds, and the wise men all together around the manger in a stable are not entirely correct. The magi were probably a few months later than the shepherds.

Getting Personal — *Has there been a time in your life when you were seeking Jesus, but didn't know where to find Him? To whom did you go for help? Did you receive good advice and instruction?*

When the magi got ready to go home, why did they take a detour? (Matthew 2:12) *they were warned in a dream not to return to Herod*

Mary, Joseph, and Jesus also took a long detour on their way back to Nazareth. Where did they go, and why? (Matthew 2:13-15)
they went to Egypt because Joseph was warned by the Lord to flee

What happened while they were gone? How did they finally know it was OK to go back home? (Matthew 2:16-23) *baby boys in & around Bethlehem were killed by Herod's men — an angel appeared to Joseph after Herod died*

Growing Up God
Read Luke 2:40-52.
As Jesus grew, what kind of child was He? (Luke 2:40, 52)
wise

In what ways was Jesus a "normal" child? (Luke 2:41-51)
he was often with friends
he was obedient

16

In what ways was Jesus unlike most other kids?

he was able to talk with the teachers in the temple + answer their questions

Read John 1:1-14.

So far, most of the references to Jesus' coming to earth have come from Matthew and Luke. Mark hardly deals with Jesus' childhood at all. And while John doesn't really deal with His childhood, he does provide a different perspective than the "baby in a manger" approach. What words did John use to describe Jesus? (John 1:1-5) *"the Word" — God, with God in the beginning*

What was Jesus' relationship with God? (John 1:2) *He was in the beginning with God*

What was Jesus' relationship with John the Baptist? (John 1:6-9) *John was the witness to the light of Christ*

What is Jesus' relationship with anyone who will receive Him? (John 1:10-13) *to all who received him + believed in his name, he gave the power to become children of God*

According to John, what is the real significance of the Christmas story? (John 1:14) *that the word became flesh + people have seen the glory of God as a person*

Getting Personal — *Consider your early childhood as you think about these questions: What was your relationship to God? What significance did Christmas have in your life?*

JOURNEY INWARD

John wrote that Jesus "came to that which was His own, but His own did not receive Him" (John 1:11). Only a few people were willing to look past the human form of Jesus to see that He was indeed the Son of God. But for those who did, the rewards were great. Even today some people look at Jesus and see rules, boredom, and legalism. Others see love, acceptance, and eternal life. So we need to spend a little time considering **your relationship with Jesus.**

From the first few days of Jesus' life, people had to make major decisions about what to think of Him. That was true throughout His life and is still true today. And even from the opening pages of the New Testament, God makes it clear that everyone is invited to receive the joy that Jesus can provide. For example, review the types of people who were present during the first Christmas. For each category, think through (1) How the people heard about Jesus; (2) What actions they took based on that information; and (3) What they had to sacrifice (or leave behind) to be present to celebrate the birth of Jesus. The first one is done for you as an example. (You may not find an answer for all of the sections.)

PEOPLE	HOW THEY HEARD	ACTIONS THEY TOOK	WHAT THEY SACRIFICED
Angels	They knew because they had a heavenly perspective	They did all God told them and spread the good news to others	The glory of heaven and the privilege of being with God the Father
Shepherds	angels	went to see	left sheep (job)
Magi (Wise men)	star	" " "	left home
Mary and Joseph	angel	parented	reputation, own family life
King Herod	Magi	had others try to find	
Anna/ Simeon	God	blessed child	

From the previous chart, you should be able to see that people found their way to Jesus through a number of ways. Some received a direct revelation and acted on it. Others used a more intellectual approach and arrived at the same place. King Herod decided to let other people do his legwork for him, so he missed out on the whole thing. And perhaps the best examples were

Anna and Simeon, who did nothing special. They were faithful to God every day, and were eventually rewarded for their faithful obedience.

Now plug yourself into the picture. What is your own relationship with Jesus like? Put an "X" on each of the lines below at the appropriate point to describe that portion of your relationship.

Emotional ....X................... Intellectual

Fresh Daily ....X........... Kind of Stale

Consistent ....X............ Up and Down

Active ....X.................................... Dormant

Confident ....X.. Uncertain

Don't worry too much if you can't truthfully check all the positive attributes you'd like. During the next 11 sessions, you'll be taking a close look at the life of Jesus. You'll probably be reminded of many of the things you have forgotten, have never known, or have become too familiar with. But the place to start is here, with an honest evaluation of your relationship with Jesus.

Before ending this session, spend some time in prayer. If you've let your relationship with Jesus slip a little, renew it. If you're not sure of your relationship with Him, promise to take an honest look at His character as you go through this book. And if everything's going fine with your relationship, then you should have plenty to pray about anyway. Make your goal for the next few weeks to be more like Jesus, who "grew in wisdom and stature, and in favor with God and men" (Luke 2:52).

 KEY VERSE

"The Word became flesh and lived for a while among us. We have seen His glory, the glory of the One and Only Son, who came from the Father, full of grace and truth" (John 1:14).

Sometimes you can take a number of perfectly capable and well-adjusted individuals for whom no challenge is too great, require them to work together in a group, and discover that they can't complete the simplest of projects.

2

TEAM(S) WORK

(Jesus: His Preparation for Ministry)

Margo could hardly believe it. After six months of working with soap and detergent clients, her boss at the advertising agency was finally giving her a chance to compete with the creative team from a competitor's agency for a new, exciting sportswear account. And what's more, the boss had given her an unlimited budget and told her to put together her own creative team.

Margo was confident she could win the account. She had worked very hard the past year, and it showed. The long overtime hours spent designing and redesigning ads was finally paying off. Her eye for color and her skill in crafting words were coveted by others in the company.

But when Margo began the project, she quickly opted to single-handedly win the account. Most of the people available to work with her on a creative team seemed inexperienced. Ignoring her boss' instructions to research past ad campaigns as well as the suggestions and offers of help from coworkers, Liz and Bob, she forged ahead.

Several days before the presentation to the client, Margo's boss stopped by to see the progress of her creative team. As he looked over the first attempts at ads, he couldn't believe his eyes.

"This is great, Margo. I really like this concept. Too bad it's already been used. Didn't you run this by Liz and Bob? Last year they put together a fantastic plan for the Wilson account using this same idea." Margo was frantic. She was counting on her concept impressing the boss. Sure enough, he was impressed, but not in the way she had handled (or mishandled) the campaign. Because Margo had refused help and suggestions, her presentation to the client was limited to several weak ideas. The client didn't even wait to respond. Margo lost the account.

A year earlier, Margo's campaign *would* have won the sportswear account. But without having all the available information, Margo made a bad mistake by ignoring her boss' instructions. The boss didn't really want to fire Margo since she did quality work, but Margo's coworkers gave her the cold shoulder treatment for several days. They had tried to tell her that her concept had been used, but she had made it clear that she didn't want *their* help.

Teams are interesting to watch. Sometimes you can take a number of perfectly capable and well-adjusted individuals for whom no challenge is too great, require them to work together in a group, and discover that they can't complete the simplest of projects. Other times, you can put together a group of individuals who can't individually tie their own shoes without Velcro, and they will come up with brilliant ideas and insights. In other words, when individuals come together and continue to act as individuals, conflict and wasted time is sure to occur. But when individuals come together and unite as a team, there's no limit to their potential.

 JOURNEY ONWARD

Jesus could have come to earth in a number of ways. He could have come riding out of the sky on a great white horse. He could have beamed Himself down to one of the heavily populated Roman arenas and announced that He was there to save the sins of the world. But instead of flying in as a heavenly ambassador who was "here today and gone-tomorrow," He decided to develop a team who could carry on His work after He was gone.

You met part of the team in the last session. Mary was selected to bring the Christ Child into the world, and she and Joseph were responsible for His well-being while He was young. The angels announced His birth. Shepherds and wise men were included in the celebration. And in this session you will see that as Jesus got older, He continued to build His team.

Read Malachi 4:5-6.
One of His primary teammates was John the Baptist, who was introduced
briefly in Session 1. He was called to pave the way for Jesus and His
ministry. And by the time Jesus began His earthly work, John already had an
active ministry of his own. The Jewish people were looking for a forerunner
to their Messiah, but they weren't looking for a "John." Whom were they
expecting? *Elijah*

Read Mark 1:1-5.
What job did John have? Do you think he would be popular in your neighborhood? In your office? *Baptizing   no   no
(because of how he looked + acted)*

Read Matthew 3:7-10.
How did he get along with the religious authorities of his time?
*not well - he called them vipers + implied
they were bad fruit + unworthy*

Read Luke 3:10-14.
What kinds of advice did he give the people? *to share + not
to cheat people*

Read John 1:19-23.
Some people thought that because of all he was saying and doing, that John
the Baptist might be the Christ they had been waiting for. How did he
handle his questioners? *He answered their questions
briefly + then explained he was the voice
crying in the wilderness as Isaiah had foretold*

While John was baptizing the people, Jesus went to him to be baptized.
What happened at this meeting? (Matthew 3:13-17) *John said
Jesus should baptize him, but Jesus insisted
on doing it the other way. as he was baptized,
the heavens opened, a dove descended + God
spoke.*

Read Matthew 4:1-11.
We know very little about Jesus' life between His birth and baptism. But His

23

baptism was kind of a sign that He was getting ready to begin His public ministry. What else did He do before He started His ministry? How long did this activity take? (Matthew 4:1-2) *He went to the wilderness + fasted 40 days + nights. The devil then tempted Him, but Jesus would not yield.*

The devil made three suggestions to tempt Jesus to listen to him. List the devil's temptations below and record Jesus' response after each one. You'll find all these recorded in Matthew 4:3-11.

TEMPTATION	RESPONSE
#1 *Command the stones to be loaves of bread*	*One does not live by bread alone but by every word that comes from the mouth of God*
#2 *threw himself off the top of the temple + have angels save him*	*Do not put God to the test*
#3 *Offered him all the kingdoms of the world.*	*Worship + serve God only*

You may have been quick to notice the substance of what Jesus said in each of the above instances, but don't overlook the little phrase He used in each of His answers: "It is written." For each one of Satan's temptations, Jesus had a ready answer from His knowledge of Scripture. All of His responses came from the Book of Deuteronomy (8:3; 6:16; 6:13). As you go through the next several sessions and see the power that Jesus had at His command, keep in mind that He was able to withstand the best the devil could throw at Him because He knew and believed the Word of God.

On the Road
Read Luke 4:14-44.
After His baptism and temptation, Jesus began to become a public figure. As He went back to His home (Nazareth), how was He received at first? Why? (Luke 4:14-15)

But as much as everyone liked Jesus' teaching, they weren't quite prepared to learn something very important that He wanted them to know. What specific teaching caused friction between Jesus and His hometown crowd? (Luke 4:16-27)

What really confused them about Jesus' wisdom? (Luke 4:22)

How did Jesus avoid an ugly incident in Nazareth? (Luke 4:28-30)

From Nazareth, Jesus went to Capernaum. He taught the people there, and they were also impressed with what He had to say. Why? (Luke 4:31-37)

What happened there that clued the people into the fact that Jesus was someone special? How old was Jesus at this time? (Luke 3:23)

What did Jesus say His mission was? (Luke 4:42-44)

Fishermen and Other Farfetched Followers
Read John 1:35-51.
During this time, Jesus was assembling a team to help Him. How did He get in touch with His first disciples? (John 1:35-42)

Not all of the people Jesus called were immediately enthusiastic about following Him. Some were fairly willing to give it a try, but why was Nathanael a little reluctant? (John 1:43-46)

What did Jesus do to help convince Nathanael to go along with Him? (John 1:47-51)

Read Luke 5:1-11.
What really convinced Simon, James, and John to drop what they were doing to follow Jesus? (Luke 5:1-11)

The instruction, "Let down your nets into deep water," sounds simple enough. But perhaps these seasoned fishermen were hesitant to act on the "whim" of a carpenter-turned-preacher. Even so, they did what Jesus asked. And what did the result cause them to discover about themselves? (Luke 5:8)

Getting Personal — *If you had been one of these people, do you think you would have made the same decision to drop everything and follow Jesus? Why or why not?*

Read Mark 2:13-17.
Jesus challenged another of His disciples to drop what he was doing and come along. Who was he, and what was his occupation? (Mark 2:13-14)

Even at this early stage of Jesus' ministry, the religious leaders were being confused by His teachings. They knew Jesus had a strong knowledge of the Scriptures and a new way of teaching that captured the attention of the people. They had witnessed several of His miraculous healings. They had probably heard (or heard about) John the Baptist's testimony about Jesus. But what was it that Jesus did that really befuddled the religious leaders? How did Jesus answer them? (Mark 2:15-17)

Read Mark 3:13-19.
Jesus continued to assemble His team until He had 12 main followers, whom He appointed as apostles. (They are also commonly referred to as the 12 disciples, though Jesus had many disciples besides these men.) List the names of the apostles below.

In addition to the 12 names, notice some of the details. Jesus renamed one of His disciples. (You'll find out why in Session 9.) He nicknamed 2 others "Sons of Thunder," which gives us a clue to their personalities. Another was a "zealot," which might infer that he was hardworking and devoted about his religious beliefs. Or it might be a reference to the organized revolutionary group known as the Zealots, whose main goal was to get the Romans out of Palestine even if it took violence to do so. Still another of Jesus' disciples is referred to simply as the one "who betrayed Him."

If you're thinking that it seems that Jesus handpicked a group of losers to assist Him in His ministry, you're not too far from the truth. As you get to know the disciples better in the next several sessions, your suspicions will probably be confirmed. But then it's also kind of encouraging to see that Jesus didn't give everyone a performance review and evaluation before He considered them disciples. He saw beyond what they were (simple fishermen, fighting brothers, outcast tax collectors, militant rebels, doubting followers, etc.) to what they could become. He still does. When He thinks of us, He doesn't so much focus on the limitations as the potential. He doesn't care that we're not as rich, good-looking, tall, slim, or talented as someone else. But He does care whether or not we're willing to follow Him. If we are, He will take care of everything else that matters.

 JOURNEY INWARD
Jesus was an excellent teacher not only because of what He taught, but also because of His consistency in modeling the principles He was teaching. He could have chosen to associate with the "upwardly mobile" people of His day—the wealthy or the religious leaders. But instead He chose to demonstrate what He wants us to do. So review some of Jesus' insight on **teamwork** and compare His attitudes to yours.

(1) Jesus was capable of doing what He needed to do without anyone's help. But He chose to involve other people in His life — for their benefit as much as for His. He showed that social interaction was important as well as individual development.

(2) Jesus didn't "toot His own horn." He was satisfied to do His work and let John the Baptist and others do the talking about Him. He did state clearly on several occasions that He is the Son of God, but His straightforward proclamation of truth was never boastful.

(3) While Jesus was putting together His team, He didn't exclude any particular group of people. He didn't seek out the rich and famous, though He didn't automatically rule them out either.

(4) As hard as we try to avoid the obvious fact, we need to admit that Jesus knows more than we do. We must learn (like Peter, James, and John in their boats) that if He asks us to do something, we should obey. Even if His request sounds silly. Even if we don't feel like it. Even if it's a little inconvenient. Jesus has already been through trials and temptations that we can't even imagine. So we should yield to His knowledge and experience if we want to avoid problems in our lives.

If you've answered truthfully, you should by now have a good idea of your capacity for teamwork and which specific areas need the most work. This would be a good time for you to stop and ask God to help you follow more closely the model of teamwork that Jesus set for us.

And why not set some goals for yourself based on each of the four areas you just responded to? For example:

(1) Why not share yourself with someone this week? Teach your employee a new facet of his or her job. Visit an elderly friend. Or just spend some time with your children. Think of some ways you can spend some time with others for their benefit. List some possibilities below.

(2) Instead of promoting your own accomplishments this week, list some other people you can build up. Beside each name, include the qualities of that person that you can honestly compliment.

(3) Who are some "left out" people that you know? List some people you can befriend this week and some specific things you can do with those people.

(4) Think again about the "hard to control" areas of your life that you listed previously. What are some steps you can take to again allow Jesus to have control of those areas?

Teamwork isn't always easy, but it's part of the lifestyle that Jesus promoted while He was on earth. More will be said about that lifestyle in the next session. In the meantime, put your goals into action this week and see for yourself—teams work!

 KEY VERSE

" 'Come, follow Me,' Jesus said, 'and I will make you fishers of men.' At once they left their nets and followed Him" (Matthew 4:19-20).

"And I promise to support and work for all people, especially the homeless."

3

LIFESTYLES OF THE POOR
AND NAMELESS

(Jesus: His Sermon on the Mount)

It's November and time for Presidential elections. Candidate A just delivered his campaign speech to convince Americans to elect him as President. And it was a terrific speech. He promised he would support a national health plan, the slowing of inflation, and more low-interest government loans. He even suggested that we consider disrupting meetings of Congress to "show them that we have the right to help choose the destiny of our country." But what really got the crowd excited was Candidate A's promise to support a proposal that would eliminate Federal Income Taxes. The cheers and applause from the crowd at the election rally went on for 10 minutes.

Suddenly Candidate B begins speaking and you are jolted back to reality as you hear the ooohs and aaahs from the crowd.

"My fellow Americans, we need to respect those in authority and set good examples to each other. If Congress loads us up with taxes, we should pay them joyfully. If health benefits continue to rise and no national health plan is made available, we should be happy to budget these expenses in our family incomes. You can be happy even though inflation rises. You can be happy even though you are unable to get a mortgage for a home."

You're ready to laugh Candidate B off the platform, but you notice that he has captured the attention of the crowd. This is new stuff they are hearing, and they are giving his words some serious thought—even though they don't fully understand what he's trying to tell them. You have to admit that

Candidate B's words will probably have a more lasting effect on the crowd than Candidate A's speech.

JOURNEY ONWARD

When Jesus began to teach, it didn't take long for most people to discover that He was quite different from any teacher they had ever known. For one thing, He spoke with a kind of certainty that they weren't used to hearing (Matthew 7:28-29). Second, He backed up His words with actions in the form of miracles—healing, control over nature, even raising people from the dead. (More on Jesus' miracles in Sessions 5 and 6.) And third, the very things that Jesus taught were so unusual that they usually called for an immediate reaction. No, they weren't unusual in the same way that some people today are unusual. Jesus was never recorded as saying, "Send me all your money and I'll personally ask God to reward you"; "Let me tell you who God wants you to vote for in the next election"; or "Here are the 10 secret steps to wealth, fame, and power."

Rather, Jesus seemed to have an entirely different perspective on daily living and its relationship to eternal things. He spoke of having love for one's enemies. Rejoicing in persecution. Developing a greater level of righteousness than the trained religious leaders (who spent their entire lives developing "righteousness"). So when Jesus taught, His listeners were usually confused, but intrigued.

And perhaps nowhere are Jesus' teachings compiled and crystallized any better than in His "Sermon on the Mount." In this session, we want to take a look at Matthew 5–7 and examine what Jesus was telling His followers to do. It will take you about 5 or 10 minutes to read straight through, but a lifetime to absorb and apply.

Read Matthew 4:23–5:1.
Jesus didn't just walk up to a bunch of strangers and hit them with a weird sermon. The crowd of people who were listening were anxious to hear every word Jesus was saying. Why were they so eager?

Jesus started by describing eight kinds of people who would be "blessed." The word *blessed* in this context is often translated "happy," but it's obviously not a kind of happiness that depends on outward circumstances. The meaning is more of an inner joy experienced by those who allow God to work in their lives and receive the peace He has to offer.

Getting Personal—*Do you feel blessed? Happy? Why or why not?*

Read Matthew 5:1-10.
List each of the eight groups of people, and give the reason they can feel "blessed."

TYPE OF PEOPLE	WHY THEY WILL BE BLESSED
#1	
#2	
#3	
#4	
#5	
#6	
#7	
#8	

Read Matthew 5:11-20.
If you couldn't find any of the previous categories that applied to you, Jesus added another way to be "blessed." He said that whenever you are insulted or persecuted for taking a stand for Him, you can be considered "blessed." Why can you be glad about such persecution? (Matthew 5:11-12)

And in case you were wondering whether or not you really *want* to be "blessed" in the manner that Jesus was describing, He tried to explain that it isn't an option for anyone who wants to follow Him. What two examples did He use to illustrate that such a lifestyle should be only natural for anyone who wishes to be His disciple? What point was He trying to make? (Matthew 5:13-16)

Lest anyone misunderstand or misinterpret what Jesus was teaching, He made it very clear that He wasn't trying to disagree with anything that they had been taught from the Mosaic Law. He hadn't come to do away with anything, but to fulfill everything. And what did He say that really must have floored most of His listeners? (Matthew 5:20)

At this time, many of the Jewish religious leaders were known as Pharisees. They were a very strict (and usually stuffy) group of men. They thought of themselves as "religious" to the extent that they tried to avoid contact with other non-Pharisees as much as possible. (*Pharisees* means "separated ones.") They taught in the synagogues and were self-proclaimed experts when it came to religious matters. They weren't all bad guys, but a lot of them had become hypocritical and judgmental because of their vast knowledge and interpretation of religion and law. So for Jesus to tell His uneducated listeners that they couldn't enter the kingdom of heaven unless their righteousness surpassed that of the Pharisees was bound to confuse them. What do you think Jesus meant by His statement?

A New Old Idea
Read Matthew 5:21-32.
In the next section of the Sermon on the Mount, Jesus addressed a number of laws that most of the people were probably familiar with. But He provided an interpretation of those laws that was quite different from anything the people had previously been taught. For example, He reminded the people that it was wrong to murder someone else. But how did Jesus' definition of "murder" differ from the courts of that time? What suggestions did Jesus provide to help us avoid this common type of murder? (Matthew 5:21-26)

[NOTE: *Raca* was a word used in approximately the same way we would use "Bonehead." The Sanhedrin was the high court of the Jews, consisting of chief priests, elders, and teachers of the Law.]

How did Jesus redefine the common concept of adultery? (Matthew 5:27-28)

And by the way, just because Jesus used a masculine example doesn't mean His definition doesn't apply to women as well. What was His simple solution for avoiding adultery? (Matthew 5:29-30)

Wait just a minute before you get the knife and begin to discard body parts. The point Jesus was trying to make here was not to actually mutilate your body to prevent lust. Rather, Jesus was stating quite emphatically that it would be better to lose a body part than to go to hell because of your lust. So if we are allowing our eyes to gaze lustfully at other people, at porno magazines, or films, etc., it would be much better to act as if we were blind.

Another problem that is common today was addressed by Jesus — divorce. Even in Jesus' day, the grounds for divorce were being loosened to the extent that men were sometimes granted divorces because their wives accidentally burned dinner while cooking. But what was the only reason Jesus gave for allowing divorce to take place? (Matthew 5:31-32)

About Those "Little" Sins...
Read Matthew 5:33-48.
Perhaps there were people (like you?) in Jesus' audience who thought that they didn't really need to hear instructions concerning murder, adultery, or divorce. If so, the next part of the Sermon on the Mount gets down to a common level that affects everyone. What were Jesus' next instructions to His listeners? (Matthew 5:33-37)

Getting Personal—*What are some of the oaths that you occasionally use?*

What was Jesus' teaching concerning revenge? (Matthew 5:38-42)

Why should we show love toward our enemies? (Matthew 5:43-48)

Do you think Jesus really expects us to be perfect? (Matthew 5:48) Explain your answer.

Read Matthew 6:1-34.
Jesus wanted His listeners to know the difference between genuine concern for others and mere pretense. He wanted His followers to live by a higher standard than the rest of the world. And it was not only on their personal relationships that they were to focus. Jesus knew that their worship practices needed a lot of improvement as well. For each of the following worship habits, summarize the right way and the wrong way to do them.

CATEGORY	WRONG WAY	RIGHT WAY
Giving to the Needy (Matthew 6:1-4)		
Prayer (Matthew 6:5-15)		
Fasting (Matthew 6:16-18)		

Getting Personal—*Have you acquired any bad worship habits?*

Why should Jesus' followers have a different set of priorities from other people? (Matthew 6:19-24)

The things that Jesus was saying were likely to raise a lot of questions from His listeners. "If I don't store up treasures, how will I buy groceries tomorrow?" "What will happen when I get old and need retirement money?" "How will my kids feel about me if I can't buy them the most popular brand of running sandals?" But Jesus didn't want His listeners worrying about all these things. What two examples did Jesus use to show people that God cared for them? (Matthew 6:25-30)

Why is it senseless for God's people to worry about material things? (Matthew 6:31-32)

How can we be assured that God will provide everything we need? (Matthew 6:33-34)

Read Matthew 7:1-29.
And just as we are challenged to avoid worry, we are also commanded to avoid judging others. What did Jesus teach about "seeing" the faults of other people? (Matthew 7:1-5)

Getting Personal — *When was the last time you had a judgmental attitude?*

But Jesus didn't want anyone to get the wrong impression about God. He knew He was asking a lot by telling His listeners not to worry, not to judge others, and to focus more on accumulating "treasures in heaven" rather than "real" money. Jesus knew more about God the Father than anyone else.

He knew that God wanted to give good gifts to His people. How did Jesus illustrate His point? (Matthew 7:7-12)

And recognizing that not everyone would be up to the challenge, Jesus encouraged His listeners to stay on the "narrow road" and enter at the "narrow gate" (Matthew 7:13-14). In other words, you can't go barreling through life, following the upwardly mobile crowd, and still maintain the level of righteousness that Jesus was speaking of. One of the problems is that too many people out there are willing to mislead you. To what did Jesus compare such people? (Matthew 7:15)

How can you tell sincere people from the ones who would do you harm? (Matthew 7:16-20)

How can someone be sure of entrance into the kingdom of heaven? (Matthew 7:21-23)

The Sermon on the Mount ends with a familiar parable. But in the context of what Jesus has been saying, what do you think Jesus wanted His listeners to learn from the parable? (Matthew 7:24-27)

How did all the people respond to these things that Jesus had been saying? (Matthew 7:28-29)

 JOURNEY INWARD

As you can see, the things that Jesus taught in His Sermon on the Mount were new ideas for those people. Actually, they are *still* new ideas. Two thousand years after the Sermon on the Mount, most people still don't love their enemies. Their lives are full of worry. They struggle to accumulate material things and give little if any thought to their eternal futures. So the Sermon on the Mount is as relevant today as it was the day it was first given. And there is much that we should absorb pertaining to our **lifestyles.**

Instead of evaluating your lifestyle based on your own opinions, try something a little different this time. Since the Sermon on the Mount is such a good "yardstick" to see how Christians should interact with the rest of the world, try to evaluate your lifestyle as an impartial observer would. Imagine that someone has been watching you closely for the past month (without your knowledge). What kinds of observations would this person have made about you in each of the following categories? Assume that the following is the notebook of your observer. What would this person have written about you?

❏ *Level of happiness* (Based on being poor in spirit [dependent on God rather than self], mournful [repentant, rather than full of pride], meek, hungry for righteousness, merciful, pure in heart, peacemaking, and persecuted because of righteousness)

❏ *Being "salt" and "light" in a wicked world*

❏ *Angry words*

❏ *Lustful thoughts*

❏ *Oaths/swearing*

❏ *Revenge*

❏ *Love for enemies*

❑ *Giving to needy*

❑ *Praying*

❑ *Fasting*

❑ *Worrying*

❑ *Judging others*

❑ *Total dependence on God*

What do you think an unknown watcher would think of you after checking you out for a month or so? Sometimes an observer's opinion of us might be quite different than *our* opinions of ourselves. And it's important to remember that we are observed by others—even when we don't realize it. As you go through the next few days, try to keep in mind the challenges contained in the Sermon on the Mount. The more you try to live according to Jesus' teaching, the clearer it will become that it can be very difficult to live a simple lifestyle. But it is important that Christians get their lives in order if they want to influence others (and relating to others is the topic of the next session). So get busy this week and try to start bringing your lifestyle into agreement with the model in the Sermon on the Mount. As you do, great will be your reward in heaven. Your life on earth won't be too shabby either.

 KEY VERSE

"Let your light shine before men, that they may see your good deeds and praise your Father in heaven" (Matthew 5:16).

Sometimes we tend to label people without taking into consideration the fact that they might have problems that we know nothing about.

4

A FRIEND INDEED

(Jesus: His Relationships)

Ashley was participating in her favorite hobby—gossiping about other people. This time her companion was Barb (the only person in a group of five who hadn't thought of a reason to leave as soon as Ashley appeared.

"Hi, Barb. Where's everyone else going?"

"Hello, Ashley. I guess they had other things they had to do."

"That's OK. But I was hoping to get some advice."

Yeah, fat chance, Barb thought. *The only time you've taken advice from anyone was when a fortune cookie told you to spend more time with your own concerns than the needs of others.* But what Barb said was: "I'm sorry. Can I help you, Ashley?"

"I can't understand why some people are so unfriendly to me. For instance, that new account executive, Doug, never smiles at me. Even when I've just checked my makeup and hair, brushed and flossed my teeth, and smiled my most charming smile, Doug hardly responds to me. It's not like I want him to be my closest friend, but he should be nicer to me. What do you think is wrong with him, Barb?"

"He might have his mind on other things, Ashley. From what I hear, Doug's wife has an alcohol problem. It's probably hard for him to act like nothing's wrong when he's around other people."

"Well, I guess that excuses Doug for not being nice to me. But Mona's another story. She hardly says hello to me anymore. We used to spend lunch hours together. I think she's becoming a snob."

"No, Ashley, Mona's not a snob. But her husband just got laid off at the factory where he had worked for 14 years, so Mona is working two part-time jobs to help out with the family finances. She probably just doesn't have time to spend with you these days."

"Oh, Barb, you just take up for everybody. But let me tell you about Old Mrs. Harper. Not even you will be able to excuse her behavior. Just as she was coming in from the parking lot, I went out of my way to flatter, uh, compliment her on the suit she was wearing. She just stared at me and walked on by. She never smiled or anything."

"Ashley, didn't you read the bulletin board? Mrs. Harper's son was in a serious accident last weekend. Maybe she was getting back from the hospital."

"Well that's no reason for her to ignore me. Barb, I just can't understand why no one wants to be my friend."

You may have noticed that Ashley is a little too caught up with herself to be sensitive to the feelings of others. But if we're truthful, all of us are some-what like her from time to time. That is, we all tend to form opinions about others based on limited knowledge. We label people "losers" or "snobs" or "loners" without taking into consideration the fact that they might have problems that we know nothing about. And our relationships with those people suffer.

But Jesus didn't have that problem. He knew everything there was to know about people — their thoughts, their weaknesses, and all of their past sins. Yet He loved them anyway and didn't let their problems interfere with His relationship with them. In this session, we want to look at several of Jesus' relationships and see what principles can help in our own relationships.

 JOURNEY ONWARD

One of the best illustrations to show how Jesus related to people was His encounter with the Samaritan woman at the well. John 4:1-8 provides the setting. Some people have commented how unusual it was for 12 people to go buy food for 13, but it allowed Jesus to have a private discussion with this lady. In most of this woman's relationships with Jewish people, she would have had three strikes against her: (1) She was a woman, which didn't carry a lot of weight in this culture; (2) She was a Samaritan—a member of a race of people whose history began when the Assyrians intermarried with the Israelites who didn't get taken into exile. Samaritans were generally despised by the Jews; and (3) She wasn't even a good moral woman, as you will see later in this story.

Read John 4:1-32.
What shocking question did Jesus ask this woman? (John 4:7)

How did the woman respond? (John 4:9)

One reason this woman may have been so amazed is that the Jewish leaders at this time promoted the idea that Samaritan women were always menstruating. So any Jewish person who touched something a Samaritan woman had touched was "unclean." Jesus knew how this woman felt. How did He turn the conversation around from His need for a drink to focus instead on the woman's need? (John 4:10-15)

What else did Jesus and the Samaritan woman discuss? (John 4:16-26)

When Jesus' disciples returned, they were all a little amazed to find Him talking with this woman, but they didn't have the courage to question Him about it (John 4:27). What was the end result of Jesus' willingness to spend some time talking to this Samaritan woman? (John 4:28-30, 39-42)

Getting Personal — *Do you think your own encounter with God was coincidental or part of God's plan and purpose for your life? If Jesus stopped by the water cooler at your work (or water fountain in your local park), what question would He ask you?*

Review John 3.
Now let's look at Jesus in quite a different setting. Go back one chapter to John 3. Who was Jesus meeting with this time, and what were the conditions of their encounter? (John 3:1-2)

The essential thing to remember in this case is that Jesus' visitor was a Pharisee — a religious leader of the Jews. What did Jesus tell him about the kingdom of God? (John 3:3)

How can you tell that Jesus' visitor was more than a little confused? (John 3:4)

Jesus compared God's Spirit to the wind — both are things that cannot be seen, yet you can certainly recognize that they are present and can determine their effects. But Jesus' guest still didn't understand. Though he was a knowledgeable teacher of Jewish Law, what was the best question this man could ask Jesus? (John 3:9)

Getting Personal — *How would you compare your own search for God with Nicodemus' search? What questions would you ask Jesus?*

Read John 3:10-21.
Summarize the rest of what Jesus told this man.

The account of this man ends rather abruptly. But remember his name, because you'll discover more about him before you finish this book.

Surprise Reactions
Jesus seemed to have a positive impact on whomever He met. But there were times when a relationship with Jesus had other, not-so-positive results. We will look at Jesus' miracles in the next two sessions, but one should be examined here because the miracle is perhaps not as noteworthy as the relationship.

Read John 9:1-41.
A man had been born blind. Jesus' disciples saw him and wondered who had sinned—assuming that either the man or his parents had provoked God in some way that resulted in a punishment of blindness. How did Jesus answer their question? (John 9:1-5)

What did Jesus do for the blind man? (John 9:6-7)

You would think that when a man born blind was suddenly able to see, that everyone would be happy for him. But instead, it seems that the man's recovery was a source of conflict for lots of people. Read John 9:8-34 and list the people who experienced some sort of conflict or confusion over the man's healing.

Due to the circumstances of the man's healing, he had never seen Jesus. All he could attest to during his questioning was: "I was blind but now I see!" (John 9:25) And while this should probably have been the most wonderful day of his life, he suddenly found himself at odds with his neighbors, the religious leaders, and his own parents. He even got kicked out of the synagogue, which was a severe and humiliating punishment. What did Jesus do when He heard what had happened to the man? (John 9:35-41)

You might think it was enough that Jesus had miraculously cured this man from his lifelong affliction. But Jesus cared about the man's inner feelings, not just his physical well-being. And even without the support of friends, family, or church, the man discovered that the support of Jesus was all he really needed. Through this account, we see that Jesus is no hit-and-run healer concerned only about our church attendance or general health. He seeks a personal, growing relationship with everyone.

And what He expects from you might surprise you somewhat. When we think of following Jesus, most likely a list of activities springs to mind: going to church, witnessing, serving other people, Bible study, and so forth. All of these activities are important. But an examination of another of Jesus' relationships helps put those things in proper perspective.

Read Luke 10:38-42.
Based on the account of Jesus' relationship with His friends Mary and Martha, what do you think He would like most from your relationship with Him?

One of the most comforting things about a relationship with Jesus is that He doesn't hold grudges. You can't do anything that He won't forgive. In fact, a lot of the Pharisees went to great lengths to make Jesus appear unlikable and unforgiving.

Read John 8:1-11.
Describe how the religious leaders tried to trap Jesus.

There was a legal basis for what the Pharisees wanted to do, but the Law was actually secondary to their cold and unforgiving attitudes toward the woman. (If they had really wanted to be legal about it, the sinful guy should have been there too!) How did Jesus sidestep the trap of the Pharisees? (John 8:7-9)

In spite of the fact that the woman had been caught in the act of an obvious sin, how did Jesus relate to her? (John 8:10-11)

Even though Jesus forgave the woman's sin and didn't try to make her feel excessive guilt, He did tell her to leave her life of sin. Why do you think He emphasized that to her?

Getting Personal — *How does Jesus' acceptance of the woman help you deal with your own sins and struggles?*

Looking Out for the Little Guy
Read Luke 19:1-10.
In addition to forgiving people who were obviously sinful, Jesus also went out of His way to love people who were obviously unloved. Zaccheus was a wealthy man, but he probably wasn't very happy. He was a short guy, so his physical appearance might not have attracted many friends. More important-ly, he was a tax collector during a time when tax collectors could charge more than necessary and keep the difference. Needless to say, Zaccheus wasn't Mr. Popularity in his neighborhood. But when Zaccheus went out of his way to see Jesus, how were his efforts rewarded? (Luke 19:1-6)

When Jesus decided to initiate a relationship with Zaccheus, how was Jesus' reputation affected? (Luke 19:7)

What positive results came from Jesus' relationship with Zaccheus? (Luke 19:8-10)

Read Mark 10:17-22.
Not all of Jesus' encounters with people had a happy ending. A different rich young man wanted to meet with Jesus on another occasion. What did he think about Jesus? (Mark 10:17)

What kind of person was he? (Mark 10:18-20)

How did Jesus feel about the young man? (Mark 10:21)

What prevented this man from establishing a relationship with Jesus? (Mark 10:21-22)

Getting Personal — *Do you ever feel as if you are trying to earn your salvation? If you were in the young man's shoes, in what area would Jesus point out that you are lacking?*

Even though this person was sad, he walked away from a relationship with Jesus. Others rejected Jesus as well, including many of the Pharisees (Nicodemus was an exception) and even His own brothers (John 7:2-5). But the people who welcomed a relationship with Him were amply rewarded for their devotion.

Jesus didn't seek out the rich, famous, and popular people to hang around with. He chose His friends like He chose His disciples — not according to what they could do for Him, but rather on what *He* could do for them.

Read Mark 10:13-16.
How did Jesus try to convince His disciples that no one was too insignificant for Him to overlook? (Mark 10:13-16)

As you have seen, Jesus didn't allow age, social status, financial condition, gender, or IQ level to determine whom He would try to befriend. When He first met people, He didn't see them as "loose" women, dishonest tax collectors, ignorant religious leaders, or people who had just been "caught in the act" during some horrible sin. It's as if He could only see the hurt that the person was experiencing. And until He had helped them remove the source of their distress, He wasn't interested in trying to preach to them about their spiritual inadequacies.

 JOURNEY INWARD

You can learn a lot about **relationships with others** by observing how Jesus treated people. And since you've already covered the written account, here's an opportunity now to review the same material visually.

No doubt you've seen weight-loss advertisements that show the before-and-after pictures of a person who has shown drastic improvement by using the sponsor's product. In this case, try to illustrate the before-and-after pictures of one of the people with whom Jesus came into contact. The "before" picture should be your idea of the person prior to his or her encounter with Jesus. The "after" picture should show how you think that person might have changed as a result of Jesus' friendship.

BEFORE	AFTER
The Samaritan woman at the well	
Nicodemus	
The blind man	
The woman caught in the act of adultery	
The rich young ruler	

If we are to try to be more like Jesus and follow the teachings He gave us in the Sermon on the Mount, we should have an effect on the people we know—both old friends and new acquaintances. How well do you stack up to Jesus in the following areas:

- ❑ Accepting everyone equally—
- ❑ Willingness to discuss spiritual things—
- ❑ Putting up with silly questions—
- ❑ Vulnerability (Openness toward others)—
- ❑ Initiating conversations—
- ❑ Lack of concern for personal advancement—

As you become more like Jesus in each of these areas, your relationships with others should blossom. Keep in mind that you are responsible for trying to reach out to others—not necessarily for their response to your efforts. Jesus allowed the rich young ruler to walk away, but only after He first offered His friendship and the opportunity for the young man to follow Him. You probably won't be able to make a difference in everyone's life, but it's still up to you to try.

As you go through this week, try to see each friend, family member, coworker, etc. you encounter as potential for a closer relationship for the good of God's kingdom. Think twice before you turn your back on the "losers." Don't be so quick to ignore the quiet people you know need friends, but who aren't that easy to be around. Be bold enough to reach beyond your usual group of friends and include some new people. Who knows? What begins as your willingness to reach out to others may "backfire" by providing you with new friendships that will last a lifetime.

 KEY VERSE

"For God so loved the world that He gave His one and only Son, that whoever believes in Him shall not perish but have eternal life" (John 3:16).

Our slogan is "If anything ever happens here, it will be a miracle."

5

OUT OF THE ORDINARY

(Jesus: His Miracles, Part I)

Good morning, ladies and gentlemen of the press, and welcome to the Grand Opening of Joe's Miracle Farm. The purpose of Joe's Miracle Farm is to create miracles. In fact, our slogan is, 'If anything ever happens here, it will be a miracle.' Now let me show you around and then I'll try to answer any questions you have.

"On your right you'll see Kevin operating our large, specially constructed cement mixer. Inside the mixer are all the individual parts of a Jaguar XJ-6 (in racing green). It's Kevin's job to keep mixing the parts and occasionally release them down the shoot. It is our belief that if he does enough mixing, one of these times the parts will mix together just right and the completed car will roll out of the machine, ready to go.

"On your left, Jan is conducting a similar experiment. She is holding a box that contains all the Scrabble letters necessary to spell out the Preamble to the Constitution. Jan draws them out one at a time, then flips them over to see what she has. So far we haven't gotten it exactly right. We've come up with some partial words to 'White Christmas,' but we're still working on, 'We the people. . . .'

"Behind you is John with our most significant experiment. He keeps mixing clay, water, and various slimy things with heat and electricity in an attempt to create life. We feel that if we hit on just the right combination of elements, we will eventually come up with something living. So far we've only come up with some gross substances.

"We have an optional tour if you're interested. In the barn down the road, a number of our people are trying to bring the dead back to life. Of course, we couldn't get a permit to work on people, so they have a collection of dead fish, assorted rodents, and roadkill. Who would like to go check it out? Don't be shy. Really. Anyone at all. No one? OK. Now, I'll take questions.

" 'Why is the strange person standing in the pond?' Good question. That's Ernie. His project is to create pontoon shoes that will allow him to walk on water. But he's still in the early stages of his research.

"You want to know about the people at the water barrels? Another good observation. They're trying to turn water into wine. We've had a little success with this experiment. So far, by adding the right ingredients, we've been able to turn water into tea, coffee, lemonade, and a number of other useful things. But we're still stuck on how to turn water into wine.

"I think we have time for one last question. 'Why am I doing all of this?' I'd like to give you the old 'Good for mankind' speech, but it wouldn't be at all true. To be absolutely truthful, I want to be famous. I want lots of money. I want my face on the covers of *Time* and *Newsweek*. And all it would take is one good miracle. So far, I've only been able to make the blind walk and the lame see, but I haven't given up. I think I'd like to be alone now. This press conference is over."

 JOURNEY ONWARD

Until Jesus' resurrection from the dead, perhaps nothing He did caused more of a stir than His miracles. The nation of Israel had the scriptural account of past leaders to whom God had given exceptional power—Moses, Elijah, Daniel, and so forth. But Jesus was no historical figure to them. He was alive and among them! And suddenly people were recognizing that perhaps they didn't have to live with their disabilities anymore. Through Jesus, there was hope and help for them.

Jesus' miracles tie in closely to His relationships that you saw in the last chapter. Even though He had tremendous, unlimited power, He never used it to show off. His miracles, like His relationships, were rooted in compassion. As you examine the miracles in this and the next chapter, keep asking yourself why Jesus performed each one.

Read John 2:1-11.
Jesus' first miracle is recorded here. What were the conditions that led to this miracle? (John 2:1-5)

What did Jesus do, and why do you think He did it? (John 2:6-10)

Note the quantity involved (v. 6—about 150 gallons!) as well as the quality (v. 10). What was the result of Jesus performing this miracle? (John 2:11)

In Session 4 you read how Jesus healed the man born blind. That was only one of many times that Jesus observed a physical need and eliminated the primary source of the problem. Many such miracles are recorded, and we have no reason to think that the Bible lists every single miracle Jesus did. The rest of this session will focus on Jesus' healing miracles, but we won't cover them all. Keep in mind that these events compose only a sample of Jesus' power.

Read Luke 5:12-16.
During the first century, leprosy was a somewhat common disease. (The Greek word translated *leprosy* could indicate a variety of skin diseases.) Lepers had to keep themselves removed from "normal" society, and if "regular" people began to get too close, the lepers were required to call out, "Unclean!" One encounter between Jesus and a leper is described in this passage. How severe was this person's leprosy? (Luke 5:12)

Exactly how did Jesus heal this "untouchable" person? (Luke 5:13)

Jesus told the man to report to the priest, which was customary procedure. (The priest would officially verify the healing.) What other request did Jesus make of the leper? (Luke 5:14-16)

Read Luke 17:11-19.
On another occasion, Jesus healed 10 lepers (at their request). What kind of response did Jesus get after His miracle? (Luke 17:11-19)

Considering the hostility between Jews and Samaritans, what is significant about this passage? (Luke 17:16)

Getting Personal — *Have you ever felt like a "leper"? Did someone "touch" you? Do you consider certain people "lepers"? How could they be touched for Christ?*

Equal-Opportunity Miracles
Read Matthew 15:21-28.
Jesus didn't limit His miracles (or His compassion) to include only the Jewish people. He usually responded to a person's faith, no matter who that person was. But sometimes He tested the person's faith a little. In the last session, you saw that He allowed what looked like a well-qualified (Jewish) disciple to walk away because he wasn't able to give up everything for Jesus. Compare that incident with the account in Matthew 15:21-28. What request did this non-Jewish woman make of Jesus? (Matthew 15:22)

How did Jesus respond to this woman's request? (Matthew 15:23-24)

When the woman persisted, how did Jesus respond? (Matthew 15:25-26)

The word translated *dogs* in verse 26 wasn't intended as an insult as much as a contrast. It suggests a pet doggie. Jesus was challenging the woman to remember that a father's duty was to tend to children before pets. Jesus had come to "His own" (John 1:11), the Jews, the "children" of God. How did this non-Jewish woman respond to Jesus' remark? (Matthew 15:27)

What resulted from her persistent conversation with Jesus? (Matthew 15:28)

Getting Personal — *With whom do you identify most in this story? The woman? The disciples? Jesus?*

This woman's story indicates that Jesus had authority over the spirit world as well as the ability to heal physical problems. A more graphic account of Jesus' control over demonic spirits is found in Mark 5:1-20.

Read Mark 5:1-20.
As Jesus' boat pulled up to shore, Jesus was approached by a man who was obviously demon-possessed. In what ways was the man at the mercy of the evil spirit? (Mark 5:1-5)

It is interesting to note that the evil spirit knew exactly who Jesus was— "Son of the Most High God." What was the name of the demon, and what was his request? (Mark 5:7-10)

What happened then? (Mark 5:11-13)

How did the people of the area respond when the once-possessed man was finally free of his evil influence and again in his right mind? (Mark 5:17)

The man who had been demon-possessed would have become a disciple on the spot, following Jesus wherever He went. But what important assignment did Jesus have for him? (Mark 5:18-20)

Read Luke 7:1-10.
Jesus was able to heal in a number of different ways. And people with large amounts of faith witnessed some very creative, but equally effective, miracles. One such person was a Roman centurion. What was the first request this person made of Jesus? (Luke 7:1-5)

As the centurion started thinking about what kind of person Jesus was, how did he modify his request? (Luke 7:6-8)

This guy deserved an A+ for his faith, and his request was granted. What did Jesus say about him? (Luke 7:9-10)

Getting Personal — *How do you handle crises similar to that of the centurion? Do you exhibit his quality of faith?*

Read Luke 8:43-48.
In another instance, a person received healing without even asking. The person performed one simple action that indicated great faith. What was this person's problem, and what was done to remedy it? (Luke 8:43-44)

Since this person sort of "stole" a miracle, how do we even know about it? (Luke 8:46-48)

He's Not Heavy, He's My Friend
Read Mark 2:1-12.
Sometimes good relationships are the starting points for miracles. For example, what if your problem was paralysis and you couldn't move on your own? How could you even get to where Jesus was so He could help you? One person with such a problem had four good buddies who carried him to Jesus. In fact, when the crowd was so thick that they couldn't get their friend close enough, what creative solution did they come up with? (Mark 2:1-4)

After all that these four guys had done to get their friend to Jesus, He didn't exactly come through with what they expected. What did Jesus tell the paralyzed man? (Mark 2:5)

The man's four friends weren't the only ones who were confused. The religious leaders immediately challenged what Jesus had said. So Jesus said something to the effect of, "I know what you're thinking. Anyone can claim to forgive sins. But healing this paralyzed man is something that can't be faked." What happened then? (Mark 2:6-12)

The Gospels are full of accounts of Jesus' miraculous healings. Many are even more incredible than the headlines of the tabloids you see in the checkout lines of your local supermarket. Read each of the following "headlines" and summarize in your own words the story of the miracle that took place.

❑ SON OF LOCAL OFFICIAL RECEIVES LONG-DISTANCE HEAL-ING (John 4:46-54)

❑ INVALID OF 38 YEARS WALKS AGAIN—Misses the boat on the healing waters, but finds cure anyway (John 5:1-15)

❑ HAND UNSHRIVELS BEFORE THE EYES OF WATCHING OFFI-CIALS (Matthew 12:9-14)

❑ WALKING TREES SIGHTED IN BETHSAIDA (Mark 8:22-26)

❑ DEMON DEFEATS DISCIPLES; STUBBORN SPIRIT SUCCUMBS TO SAVIOR (Mark 9:14-29)

❑ SABBATH HEALING SPARKS CONTROVERSY ON SYNAGOGUE FLOOR (Luke 13:10-17)

We haven't covered all the healing miracles of Jesus in this session, but you've been able to see a pretty good sample of what He was able to do. Perhaps you're thinking, *These are all wonderful stories, but how do they possibly relate to me?* Glad you asked.

 JOURNEY INWARD

The one thing you might have in common with the people who received Jesus' miracles is your **potential**. Three facts keep coming through in these stories: (1) Jesus had compassion for suffering people. He didn't enjoy seeing them either spiritually blind or physically limited in any way; (2) Jesus had the power to help these people; and (3) Jesus saw past the limitations of the people who asked for His help. It is true that He could see what they were, but more important, He could see what they might become.

As you apply these facts to your own concerns, review the types of miracles Jesus performed. The water-to-wine miracle showed His power, sure, but it also showed that Jesus cared about the social reputation of the bride and groom. He didn't want to see them humiliated in front of all their friends and family. He cast out demons to prove that He can remove anything that restricts our relationship with Him. He healed the daughter of the non-Jewish woman to show that there are no "outsiders" as far as He is concerned. He healed the centurion's servant and showed us that His power is not affected by time or space. The woman who touched the hem of His robe was healed, showing all of us how important it is to have faith in Him. All of Jesus' miracles *then* should motivate us *now*.

So think for a moment of the things that prevent you from living up to your full potential. Then suppose you saw Jesus walking down the street and you could stop Him and ask Him for a miracle. What would you ask for? Why?

Do you think Jesus would grant your request? Why or why not?

If Jesus were to do what you asked, how would your life change? Do you think your relationship with Jesus would improve, get worse, or stay the same? Explain.

If Jesus didn't do what you asked, how would your life be affected? Do you think your relationship with Him would improve, get worse, or remain the same? Explain.

Jesus wants the quality of our lives to improve. He has compassion for our sufferings. He has the power to heal. But we must take care not to develop the attitude that says, "When Jesus takes away all my problems, *then* I'll try to improve my relationship with Him." We certainly don't have the right to "blackmail" Jesus into giving us everything we want.

Sometimes God allows us to undergo unpleasant experiences to help us mature and grow (so we'll learn that He's always right there to lean on). At other times our own sin prevents us from receiving what God might want to give us. Still other times we may be suffering alone because we don't call on our friends to give us a hand. (Remember the paralyzed guy? Only when his four friends got involved was he able to have Jesus heal him.)

So to close this session, try to think of anything (possessions, attitudes, friends, etc.) that might be preventing you from receiving all that Jesus has to offer. Also come up with some steps you can take to remedy whatever problems you discover. Write your observations below.

Now ask Jesus to work in your life and help you reach your full potential even if it takes a miracle. And don't give up if you don't get what you want right away. (Session 7 will contain a parable teaching us the importance of persistent prayer.) If Jesus says yes to your request, thank Him and tell others about it. And if, for whatever reason, He doesn't give you what you ask for, you'll still discover that He's full of compassion and more than able to give you the strength to endure and overcome your problem(s). If you don't believe that now, keep working your way through this series.

 KEY VERSE

"Jesus went throughout Galilee, teaching in their synagogues, preaching the good news of the kingdom, and healing every disease and sickness among the people" (Matthew 4:23).

Would you be willing to buy tickets to a meteor shower or the sight of UFOs streaming across the sky?

6

TALES OF THE UNEXPECTED

(Jesus: His Miracles, Part II)

If you could buy tickets to journey out into the country and watch dozens of UFOs go streaking across the sky, would you do it? How much would you be willing to pay for such a sight?

If you lived in a drab, dull setting, constantly surrounded by boring scenery, what would it be worth for you to transform your locale into a shining, sparkling wonderland for a day or two? How much would you be willing to spend?

Suppose you've been having a gloomy, depressing day. What would it be worth to look up and see bright bands of bold colors streaming across the gray sky?

What if just once you could see a giant fireball go streaking overhead? Or a massive light show in the evening sky? Or an all-natural water park, with hot and cold water, jet sprays, mud pits, and not a mechanical device in sight?

While mankind hasn't been able to simulate a lot of these "unnatural" phenomena, their natural counterparts are magnificent in themselves. Instead of UFOs, try setting aside a clear night when a meteor shower is in progress. It can be quite impressive. The next time you observe a snowfall, notice how it transforms the surrounding landscape into a much more beautiful place. When the conditions are right, check out the brilliance of a rainbow against an overcast sky. The sun, that giant fireball, goes blazing across the sky every day (usually unnoticed). The stars are out every night, providing a spectacular light show for anyone fortunate to be far enough away from the glare of city lights. And a visit to Yellowstone Park will allow you to see a multitude of natural wonders that can amaze the most apathetic person.

Someone once observed that if the stars only came out once a century, there would be an incredible amount of preparation. That's probably true. Real estate in the remotest locations would become valuable. People would stumble all over each other for the best seats. Vendors would walk among the crowds hawking Milky Way candy bars and a variety of "Night of 1,000 Stars" T-shirts. Anticipation would increase as the sun finally went below the horizon and the sky turned dark. And then, the "ooooohs" and "aaaaahs" would probably be deafening as the millions of viewers stood openmouthed, staring at the sky. People would think, *This is a once-in-a-lifetime miracle*, and they would be right.

But, hey, we've all seen stars before. Right? Big deal. They're out every night. Nothing special about them. We know that the area of space over our heads is just one tiny little portion of a vast, seemingly endless universe. So who cares about a few hundred thousand stars that are light years away, yet twinkling and streaking across the sky for our viewing pleasure?

As small children, we loved to stare at the stars. We were fascinated as we watched tadpoles turn into frogs. We strolled through the crisp fall air and saw how the leaves changed into wondrous colors. We learned about genes and chromosomes, and marvelled when we discovered where babies really come from. But as we "matured," many of us completely lost our sense of the miraculous. Nothing seems to amaze us anymore.

 JOURNEY ONWARD

We aren't all that unusual in overlooking the miraculous things around us. Even when Jesus was performing tremendous miracles, His observers didn't always seem to have a proper level of wonder. As you saw in the last session, Jesus was a compassionate healer who used His power to help those who were suffering. But His actions weren't always fully appreciated (as in the case of the nine lepers who never said thanks), and His motives were often questioned by the Pharisees. There always seemed to be a few people who just refused to let Jesus' miracles have an effect on them. While the last session focused on Jesus' healing miracles, this one will center on His miracles that pertain to the laws of nature.

Read Mark 4:35-41.
How was Jesus' reaction to this situation different from that of His disciples? (Mark 4:38-39)

How did Jesus respond to that difference? (Mark 4:40)

What effect did this miracle have on Jesus' disciples? (Mark 4:41)

Getting Personal — *Do you ever feel that Jesus is asleep when you are in danger? How does this story encourage you?*

Read Matthew 14:22-36.
As amazing as this miracle was, the disciples must have been even more amazed on another occasion. The conditions were similar, but this time they were in the boat on the lake without Jesus. Why wasn't He with them? (Matthew 14:22-24)

How did Jesus catch up with His disciples? (Matthew 14:25)

And were the disciples glad to see Him? Explain (Matthew 14:26).

Since they weren't convinced Jesus was who He said He was, what foolproof test did Peter come up with? (Matthew 14:27-29)

What flaw did Peter's plan have? (Matthew 14:30-31)

What effect did this miracle have on the disciples? (Matthew 14:32-33)

At this point in His ministry, how was Jesus being received by the people? Why? (Matthew 14:34-36)

It has been obvious so far that Jesus had the power to heal any kind of disease, to overpower any force of nature, to forgive any kind of sin, and to restore anyone to fellowship with God. It should be noted at this point that Jesus had not tried to "hog" the glory or become a one-man show for the people. What had He done to continue developing teamwork among His disciples? (Matthew 10:1)

Palestine's Largest Picnics
Read Matthew 14:1-21.
Another miracle resulted because Jesus had been trying to find a place to be by Himself. Why did He want to be alone? (Matthew 14:1-13)

Why wasn't Jesus able to be by Himself? (Matthew 14:13-14)

As evening approached, the disciples reminded Jesus that they (and the large crowd of people following them) were all away from home and the nearest fast-food restaurant. What did Jesus suggest that the disciples do? (Matthew 14:15-16)

John's account of this story gives us a little more insight about why Jesus made His suggestion. He wanted to see how much faith His 12 main followers were developing. How did the disciples do on this "test"? (John 6:5-9)

After Andrew convinced the boy to share his sack lunch, what was Jesus able to do with it? (Matthew 14:17-21)

Read Matthew 15:32-38.
You would think that the disciples would get some idea of what kinds of things they would be able to accomplish with a little faith. Wrong! Not long afterward, the same situation came up. Jesus had been with great crowds of people for three days, and no one was operating a concession stand nearby. It seems that since Jesus was healing "the lame, the blind, the crippled, the dumb, and many others" (Matthew 15:30), He shouldn't have had to be responsible for everyone's eating schedule as well. But He had compassion for the people. (He didn't want to help a lame person walk, only to have the guy collapse from hunger on the way home!) So who did Jesus recruit to take care of the food situation? (Matthew 15:32)

And how did they respond to His suggestion? (Matthew 15:33)

Keep in mind that Jesus had just recently shown these guys what it was possible for Him to do. But it seems as if they hadn't learned a thing from the previous miracle. How did their initial food supply this time compare to the last time? (Matthew 15:34)

How did the number of people to feed compare to the last time? (Matthew 15:35-38)

Getting Personal—*The disciples had seen Jesus' healing. They had seen how He had control over nature. In the feeding of the masses of people, they had seen Him bypass the "laws" of science. But they had already failed a couple of times to show that they were learning anything from Jesus' miracles. If you were a disciple, how do you think you would be responding to all of Jesus' miracles at this point?*

Death-defying Acts
Read Luke 7:11-17.
And in spite of all the many wonderful things we've seen that Jesus has done so far, nothing is as phenomenal as what we're about to examine next. Jesus and His disciples had their usual large crowd following along behind them when they came upon a ceremony taking place in the town of Nain. What was happening there? (Luke 7:11-12)

This was a common ceremony. Why do you think Jesus decided to involve Himself in this case? (Luke 7:12-13)

What happened after Jesus took action? (Luke 7:14-15)

What effect did this miracle have on the people there? (Luke 7:16-17)

Read Luke 8:40-42, 49-56.
In a similar incident, a man named Jairus asked for Jesus' help. What did Jairus want Jesus to do? (Luke 8:40-42)

What was significant about Jairus asking Jesus for help? (Luke 8:41)

But before Jesus could complete the journey to Jairus' house, what news did Jairus receive? (Luke 8:49-50)

How did the people at Jairus' house respond to Jesus (the carpenter's son) when they thought He was making a medical diagnosis? (Luke 8:51-53)

What miracle did Jesus perform for Jairus' daughter? (Luke 8:54-56)

Some people try to disprove that Jesus really performed miracles. Such people might read the accounts of Jairus' daughter and the widow of Nain's son and argue that the people in those stories hadn't really died, but had just passed out. The Bible includes a third story of someone Jesus resurrected, leaving no doubt that Jesus has power over death (as well as nature, disease, science, etc.).

Read John 11:1-57; 12:9-11.
Again, Jesus was approached by a messenger. What was the situation? (John 11:1-3)

Lazarus was a close friend of Jesus. And with that in mind, Jesus' response to the message was a little unusual. How did Jesus react to the message? (John 11:4-6)

When Jesus decided to go to Judea to help Lazarus, His disciples reminded Him that the last time He was there He was almost killed. Why did Jesus insist on returning? (John 11:11-16)

What was the scene upon Jesus' arrival in Judea? (John 11:17-19)

How did people respond to Jesus when He arrived? (John 11:20-37, especially verses 21, 32, and 37)

And when Jesus started to take action, even His close friends questioned His intentions. What did Jesus say to convince everyone that they should let Him go ahead? (John 11:38-40)

What were the results of this miracle? How did it affect Jesus? (John 11:45-57)

How did the miracle affect Lazarus? (John 12:9-11)

As you can see, sometimes miracles had the desired effect—they motivated the observers to increase their faith in God and trust Him to oversee their lives. On the other hand, some people refused to recognize the miracle as being proof of God's power. They chose instead to try to overlook it, cover it up, or explain it away because the miracle threatened them in some way.

Even Jesus' disciples were kind of slow when it came to learning from His miracles. Perhaps they became so accustomed to seeing Him perform miracles that they just lost the capacity to be overwhelmed. Even when they had the opportunity to participate in a miracle (such as walking on water), they came up short in the Faith Department.

Read Matthew 17:24-27.
How did Jesus try to teach His disciples that all their needs would be provided for?

In John 21:25, we are given a valuable insight into the life of Jesus. We read that, "Jesus did many other things as well. If every one of them were written down, I suppose that even the whole world would not have room for the books that would be written." So don't limit your concept of Jesus' power to the few miracles that you've examined. They are just a starting point for trying to discover exactly what Jesus was capable of doing. And as we reflect on those few things, we should be secure in the fact that He is in complete control of all the negative forces we face.

 JOURNEY INWARD

Reading about all the miracles of Jesus won't mean a lot to us if we neglect the "common," "ordinary" evidence of God's power that we experience every day. So take a few minutes to reflect on **God's wonders in daily life.**

Don't rush this activity. Take your time. Start small. Think only about your body. *Nothing wonderful there!* you think? Don't be so sure. The very fact that you are reading these words means that your optic nerves are doing some incredible things. Your ability to read and your capacity to understand are only two of the millions of functions of your brain. As you sit there, you are breathing. Your body is taking in oxygen from the air and releasing carbon dioxide, which keeps the animal/plant balance in good working order. What other "wonders" can you list from within your body?

Now let your thinking expand a little. Think about your house or apartment complex. What miracles can you find there? Does your yard have any particularly outstanding trees or shrubs that evoke a sense of wonder in you from time to time? Does the bond you have with your family ever cause you to be thankful? As you watch the seasons change outside your window, doesn't the cycle seem a little on the miraculous side? Record all the things you can think of that might qualify as wonders.

Now think of the state or province you live in. What are the places that take your breath away? If you don't like your state, think of your country. Have you ever marveled at the giant redwood trees in California? At Crater Lake in Oregon? At the Everglades in Florida? The glaciers in Canada? Victoria Falls in Africa? The Amazon River? England's white cliffs of Dover? These places were formed by the same Creator who calmed the raging seas and fed the multitudes with five loaves and two fish. What places cause you to think of God because of their beauty or grandeur?

And if no place on earth is significant enough for you, think of the universe. It doesn't take much thought to cause even the most complacent among us to be astounded at our lives in the midst of such a vast expanse.

You see, if we take for granted all the little "miracles" that surround us, it's really hard to appreciate the fact that Jesus walked on water or raised the dead. If we refuse to acknowledge God's power in the physical world around us, we are in danger of overlooking the even more important spiritual miracles God performs (forgiveness of sin, salvation, etc.).

So today (or tomorrow at the latest) try to go through your usual routine, but keep your eyes open for little "miracles." As you begin to see more of God in your daily life, it will put a new perspective on everything you do. And when that happens, it won't take a miracle to make you a happier and more fulfilled person.

To close, memorize the key passage below. And after you memorize these words of Jesus, think about them often. How can you better demonstrate faith in Jesus? How can you possibly do "greater things" than Jesus did?

What does it mean to ask for things in Jesus' name? These verses are sometimes misinterpreted to suggest that Jesus will grant every desire we have—for money, status, etc. But when properly understood, they give an incredible promise that shows how much Jesus thinks about you.

 KEY VERSE

"I tell you the truth, anyone who has faith in Me will do what I have been doing. He will do even greater things than these, because I am going to the Father. And I will do whatever you ask in My name, so that the Son may bring glory to the Father. You may ask Me for anything in My name, and I will do it" (John 14:12-14).

Is it God's will that we disconnect our brains when we think about spiritual things?

SOMETHING TO THINK ABOUT

(Jesus: His Parables, Part I)

See how quickly you can figure out the following brainteasers. (Some will probably take awhile.) The answers are at the end of this session, but don't peek unless you have to.

(1) Four common English words end in the letters *-dous*. Can you name them?

(2) If you begin counting from the number one, how far will you have to go before you get to a number containing the letter A?

(3) If "A. S. in T. S. N" is short for "A Stitch in Time Saves Nine," what are the other quotable sayings below?

❑ The E. B. G. the W.

❑ O. G. T. D. A.

❑ The B. T. in L. A. F.

❑ S. S. and C. A. B. S.

❑ A. P. S. is A. P. E.

(4) Remove only four of the lines below to leave four equilateral triangles of the same size. There can be no extra lines or loose ends.

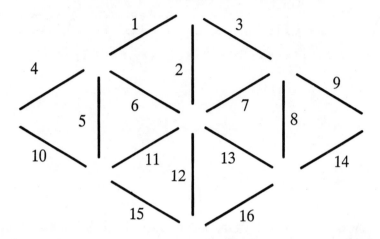

(5) Select six numbers from the following grid that will include the numerals "0" through "9" exactly once. You may not select more than one number from any row (across) or column (up and down). Here's a clue: Try to cross off any numbers that you can to narrow down your possibilities.

1	8	15	22	29	36	43
2	9	16	23	30	37	44
3	10	17	24	31	38	45
4	11	18	25	32	39	46
5	12	19	26	33	40	47
6	13	20	27	34	41	48
7	14	21	28	35	42	49

Some people enjoy brainteasers more than others. But it's important for all of us to put our brains to use as often as possible. God created us with a marvelous capacity to think and to reason.

Yet sometimes when we begin thinking about spiritual things, we tend to assume that it's God's will for us to disconnect our brains. After all, we're supposed to live by faith. Many Christians like to quote the slogan: "God said it. I believe it. That settles it." The slogan is catchy, but it might be confusing. If God says something, we should at least give it some thought before we file it into our brains. Otherwise, why has He given us such a wonderful ability to think?

Jesus didn't always come right out and give His listeners a list of facts to learn and verses to memorize. He used common objects as teaching aids. He told stories. He asked hard questions. He tried to get people to think and even to challenge their religious customs that weren't working out or that didn't make any sense.

When Jesus challenged Nicodemus to be "born again," He wasn't speaking literally. But He did want Nicodemus to grapple with this new concept for a while. If Nicodemus had thought, *Jesus said it. I believe it. That settles it* (without understanding what Jesus really meant), he would have had a world of trouble trying to do what Jesus told him.

In this session and the next, we want to look at some of Jesus' parables. In some cases, it's obvious what Jesus wants us to know. In other instances, you may need to struggle (mentally) with the parable before it begins to make sense. But you'll have the same satisfaction as when you finally solve a difficult brainteaser, crossword puzzle, or computer game.

 JOURNEY ONWARD

In this session we'll cover several of Jesus' parables concerning relationships. Session 8 will delve into His parables pertaining to the kingdom of God. We'll start with some of Jesus' easier parables. But even so, don't just give the usual pat answers. Put your brain into gear and give these parables some serious thought.

Read Luke 15:1-7.
What do you think Jesus wanted His listeners to learn from this parable?

So there could be no doubt in this case, Jesus went on to provide His own specific interpretation. What did Jesus want everyone to know? (Luke 15:7)

What information does this parable provide about your relationship with God?

Jesus made the same point using another short parable. What illustration did He use this time? (Luke 15:8-10)

And just in case His listeners were as dense as some of today's people, Jesus made the point a third time. This time He elaborated a bit. What illustration did He use this third time? (Luke 15:11-32)

Getting Personal — *Of the three major characters in this story, who are you most like? Why?*

Why do you think the father was so forgiving?

Why do you think the older brother was so unforgiving?

Read Luke 18:1-14.
Many of Jesus' parables emphasized the importance of developing a good relationship with God. And sometimes His illustrations were rather unusual. To describe the effects of praying, for instance, what analogy did Jesus use? (Luke 18:1-5)

Do you think Jesus was trying to say that we annoy God with our prayers? Explain.

What was Jesus' point in this parable? (Luke 18:6-8)

Isn't it comforting to know that Jesus was (and is) aware of the many injustices in the world? He knew that if we are persistent in our prayers, we are able to remain sure that God is in control of our lives. We aren't alone in our daily struggles. But the fact that we pray regularly is no automatic remedy for our problems. Jesus was also concerned with how we pray.

Even during the first century there were snobs who thought they were better than everyone else. So Jesus told a parable that showed that these people surely weren't fooling God. Why do you think God heard the prayer of the second person and not the first person? (Luke 18:9-14)

Getting Personal — *Which of these two characters are you more like? Why?*

Jesus was usually very severe in His comments about people who were leading hypocritical lives. One reason was probably that Jesus was constantly aware of the spiritual effects of self-righteous actions. He knew a time would come when God would separate the truly righteous people from those who were only faking it. And some of His parables tried to get this point across. One such parable is found in Luke 14:15-24.

Read Luke 14:15-35.
What do you think the banquet in this passage refers to?

One excuse you might want to include on your list is that Christianity turns out to be a little too demanding for some people. They want the initial love, forgiveness, and "warm fuzzy feelings" that Christianity has to offer, but they don't want to commit to the work, discipline, and sacrifice that come later. How does Jesus describe this attitude? (Luke 14:25-35)

Jesus repeatedly challenged His listeners to look toward the future and not just focus on the here-and-now. In fact, He warned them of severe consequences if they didn't prepare themselves spiritually. Again, a parable makes this point.

Read Luke 12:13-21.
What do you think Jesus meant to be "rich toward God"? (Luke 12:21)

Do you think Jesus is saying it's wrong to be rich? Explain.

Getting Personal — *In what ways are you like the person in this parable? Explain.*

Advance Warning

Even though many of the parables Jesus used were hard to understand, He made sure certain things were very clear. One fact He repeatedly stressed was that someday we will all undergo the judgment of God, at which time we will be held accountable for what we've done with our lives. To disregard this fact can have disastrous results.

Read Matthew 25:14-30.
Why do you think the master gave his servants different amounts of money?

Something to Think About

Do you think the master had a right to be angry with the third servant? Explain your answer.

Why do you think the master gave the third servant's talent to the one who had 10 instead of the one who only had 4?

As you can see, Jesus covered a lot of topics in parables. He was even able to talk about Himself in His parables.

Read Matthew 21:33-46.
Who do you think the following symbols represent:

❑ The landowner

❑ The tenants

❑ The landowner's servants

❑ The landowner's son

This parable wasn't too hard for the people to figure out. What did they realize was going to happen? (Matthew 21:40-41)

What effect did this parable have on the religious leaders? (Matthew 21:42-46)

Down to Earth

Jesus isn't concerned only about our relationships with God. He also wants us to work on improving our relationships with each other. It makes good sense because our relationships with each other can affect our relationships with God. To illustrate, here's another parable. And this is one of those that you might need to mull over a while before it begins to make sense.

Read Luke 16:1-7.
What would you do if you were the rich man in this story and had a manager like the one described?

When you read the next verse, you see that the rich man *commended* his manager. Why do you suppose the manager was praised for his actions?

Do you think Jesus is encouraging us to be dishonest on the job if we can't see any other way around a problem? Explain.

What did Jesus want us to learn from this shrewd manager? (Luke 16:9)

And since it's important to *develop* strong relationships with each other, it's also essential that we *maintain* those friendships. One day Peter was thinking about that very subject. He asked Jesus how often a person should be required to forgive someone for an offense. Big-hearted Peter offered to forgive an offender up to seven times. (Religious teachers during this time said that forgiving someone three times was an adequate action.)

Read Matthew 18:21-35.
What did Jesus tell Peter? (Matthew 18:21-22)

Then Jesus emphasized His point with another parable. If you read this parable from a Bible translation that uses the word *talent*, keep in mind that one talent was a weight (probably of gold) between 58 and 80 pounds. What was the original problem in this parable? (Matthew 18:23-25)

How was the problem resolved? (Matthew 18:26-27)

What was the second problem? (Matthew 18:28)

How was this problem resolved? (Matthew 18:29-30)

What was the result of the lack of forgiveness? (Matthew 18:31-34)

What did Jesus want His listeners to learn from this parable? (Matthew 18:35)

Other parables take a more positive approach as they promote the importance of helping others. One of the most familiar is the Parable of the Good Samaritan. Now that you know that Samaritans were looked down on by the Jews, you can appreciate the significance of this parable.

Read Luke 10:25-37.
Why did Jesus tell the Parable of the Good Samaritan? (Luke 10:25-29)

In what ways are you like the person who was questioning Jesus?

In what ways are you like the priest and the Levite?

In what ways are you like the Samaritan?

Getting Personal — *In what ways have you shown mercy to others this week? What opportunities have you missed?*

There's one more short parable we should look at before ending this session because it deals with forgiveness and appreciation. Jesus had been asked to dinner by a Pharisee named Simon. What happened while Jesus was there that embarrassed His host? (Luke 7:36-39)

Jesus could tell what Simon was thinking. But instead of giving him a sermon, He told him a parable. What was the point of the parable? (Luke 7:40-43)

How did this parable apply to Simon the Pharisee? (Luke 7:44-50)

Getting Personal — *How might this parable apply to you?*

The parables should encourage us to use our brains a little more than we usually do. And if we begin to use our brains when it comes to religious things, we are likely to come to several conclusions. We start to realize exactly how much we really owe God that we can never repay. We see ourselves as less significant than we usually do. We begin to understand the point of some of the things Jesus said that we've always overlooked or taken for granted. And we get a glimpse of exactly how much we still don't know.

JOURNEY INWARD

You probably found some of Jesus' parables very clear and to the point. Others were probably harder to understand. The next two sessions will contain additional information that runs toward the "difficult" side, but we should never give up on something just because we don't immediately understand it. Otherwise, why did God fill our skulls with such a wonderful organ as the brain? So spend a few minutes now considering **the thinking process.**

In the last session you were asked to list the ordinary, everyday wonders that surround you. Now take a few minutes to list some of the man-made wonders you've seen. For example, you might list television. It's so common these days to push a button, turn a knob, and have dozens of channels of information and entertainment available to you. Yet the technology that makes your television work is extremely complex. God didn't create television, but He did create mankind with brains capable of learning to transmit visual images electronically.

List some of the man-made accomplishments that boggle your mind. (Sky-scrapers? Computers? Sports cars? Picasso paintings? Classic songs? Space shuttles?) Record your list below.

All the things you listed are a result of someone using his/her mind for constructive purposes. And the people who created all those things probably started off as bored as you. It's never too late to discipline yourself to use your brain more. Think of the past three days. Approximately how much of your thinking time was focused on:

- [ ] Home-related activities   _____ %
- [ ] Job-related thoughts   _____ %
- [ ] Creative efforts (music, art, crafts, etc.)   _____ %
- [ ] Daydreaming   _____ %
- [ ] Memories about past experiences   _____ %
- [ ] Thoughts about the future   _____ %
- [ ] Worrying about various things   _____ %
- [ ] Other: _____ %
- [ ] _____ _____ %
- [ ] _____ _____ %
- [ ] _____ _____ %
- [ ] _____ _____ %

One category was intentionally left off the above list to see if you would come up with it on your own: spiritual things. Most of us spend a lot of time thinking about things that aren't necessary or beneficial. We could all profit by focusing our thoughts on God more than we usually do. When we keep God in mind, our thoughts usually find a new, healthier perspective. Since God provided us with such active brains, the least we can do is use them for Him a little more often.

So spend at least five minutes now just thinking about God—who He is, what He has done for you, what He expects of you, etc. If you're still a little fuzzy about some of the parables you've just read, go over them again and ask Him to provide wisdom. When you focus your thoughts on God, you won't need to think twice about whether or not it was a good idea.

[After you've spent some time with God, you may want to go back to your brainteasers. When you think you've got them all figured out, check your answers against these: (1) *hazardous, horrendous, stupendous,* and *tremendous;* (2) One thousand; (3) The Early Bird Gets the Worm, One Good Turn Deserves Another, The Best Things in Life Are Free, Speak Softly and Carry a Big Stick, and A Penny Saved Is a Penny Earned; (4) Remove lines 3, 7, 11, and 15; (5) To have six numbers containing a total of 10 digits, you must select four two-digit numbers and two single-digit numbers. Since the single-digit numbers could not be in the same column, one of your numbers has to be either 8 or 9. And since your four two-digit numbers will have to begin with 1, 2, 3, and 4, you can eliminate any numbers that end in those digits. So beginning with the 8 or 9, crossing out all the numbers that won't work, and looking for the zero (because there are only three possibilities), a little trial and error should lead you to discover that the correct numbers are 6, 8, 17, 25, 30, and 49.]

 KEY VERSE

"Jesus spoke all these things to the crowd in parables; He did not say anything to them without using a parable. So was fulfilled what was spoken through the prophet: 'I will open My mouth in parables, I will utter things hidden since the creation of the world'" (Matthew 13:34-35).

Mysteries require us to separate truth from fiction as we piece together just the right set of clues to find the correct solution.

THE MYSTERY UNFOLDS

(Jesus: His Parables, Part II)

You've just gotten your detective license, and it's your first day on the job. Your gorgeous (or handsome) secretary hands you three cases that your predecessor was unable to solve. Jot your impressions in each one of the case files below.

CASE #1 — A laundromat owner is frustrated that his machines are being used continually, but his money keeps coming up short. When he opens the money boxes at the end of the day, he only has about half the quarters he should, and they are all wet. What's his problem?

CASE #2 — A safe is cracked aboard a luxury yacht, and the owner's money and jewelry are stolen. The most likely suspect is a man in a sailor's uniform who says he was on shore leave. But the man testifies that: "I couldn't have broken into the safe because I only stayed in the front of the yacht for a little while and then went back to the boat where I'm stationed." What would you tell your client?

CASE #3 — A scientist is found hanging in his laboratory. He is discovered by the janitor, who testifies that the door and windows were both locked from the inside. It doesn't seem the man could have hanged himself because he is well off the floor and there is no furniture nearby. The carpet underneath the man looks as if something had sat there previously, but it is completely dry. The only peculiar thing is that the man is wearing insulated rubber boots with his lab coat. The police want to know how you think the man died.

Mysteries can be a lot of fun. They are similar to brainteasers (like you tried in the last session), yet mysteries have a distinctive difference. Like brainteasers, you need knowledge, logic, and intellect to solve mysteries. But good mysteries also require you to separate truth from falsehood, uncover hidden facts, and piece together just the right set of clues to find the correct solution.

Sometimes we discover the right combination of clues and identify the culprit long before the dramatic unveiling at the end of the story. Other times we are held in suspense right up to the last minute and have to be told how all the pieces fit together. (And to be honest, aren't the best mysteries the ones you just couldn't quite figure out in time?)

Many of Jesus' parables deal with "mysteries." Obviously, Jesus knows a lot about spiritual things that we don't. Some of the information He has is much too complicated to dump on us all at once. So Jesus transmits this information through parables and lets us absorb it a little at a time as we mature and develop in our faith. Some things we will never fully understand until we get to heaven and have it explained to us. But in most cases, we can get a pretty good grip on the meaning if we continue to work on unraveling the "mystery" (by uncovering spiritual clues).

Speaking of clues, how did you do on the opening exercises? Here are the solutions: (1) The patrons of the laundromat have learned that the owner can be easily deceived. Many of them freeze ice cubes in the shape of quarters, leaving only a puddle in the coin box; (2) A good detective would arrest the "sailor" and take him in for questioning. A real sailor's reference to the "front" of the yacht should have been "bow," and he would have gone back to a "ship," not a "boat"; (3) The man committed suicide. As a scientist, he had access to dry ice. After locking the doors and windows, he stood on the "ice" while adjusting the noose. The rubber boots were necessary to protect his feet. As the dry ice "melted," it turned to carbon dioxide gas and left him hanging without a trace.

Now let's leave behind the cheap, fictional scenarios and move on to some mysteries that are truly meaningful.

 JOURNEY ONWARD

The parables in the last session focused on relationships. In this session you will be looking at parables that Jesus told to help us understand the mysteries of the kingdom of God. Each parable is like a clue, so you might not want to make too much out of any single parable. Your perception will be much more accurate if you examine as many "clues" as possible and then put together the big picture.

Read Matthew 9:14-17.
This parable was given in response to a kind of an accusation against Jesus. What did one of the disciples of John the Baptist want Jesus to explain? (Matthew 9:14)

What do you think Jesus meant by His response? (Matthew 9:15)

Getting Personal — *Have you ever thought about the issue of fasting? Do you need to fast to follow Jesus?*

Then Jesus illustrated His statement with a parable. What two object lessons did He use to show that He was ushering in a new standard? (Matthew 9:16-17)

Jesus' comparisons would be a lot more obvious in a culture centered around agriculture and handmade goods than they might be today. But it's not too hard to see that sometimes things serve their purpose and then age to the point where they must be replaced rather than adapted.

Read Mark 4:21-23.
Jesus makes another obvious comparison in this parable. A modern version of His question might be, "When you wire your house, do you put the lights under the beds?" The answer is, "Obviously not." Why not?

What do you think was Jesus' point in telling this parable?

Getting Personal — *Are you hiding your "lamp"? If so, when do you plan to bring it out into the open?*

Now read the following short parables, think about them for a while, and explain how the kingdom of God is like:

❑ A growing seed (Mark 4:26-29)

❑ A mustard seed (Matthew 13:31-32)

❑ Yeast (Matthew 13:33)

❑ Hidden treasure (Matthew 13:44)

❏ A pearl (Matthew 13:45)

❏ A net (Matthew 13:47-50)

If you don't fully understand all of these parables after the first reading, don't be too disappointed. You can look through different Bible commentaries on these passages and find a variety of interpretations. Some of the parables are more obvious than others. And since Jesus didn't fully explain all of them, there is no way to say that one person's interpretation is completely right while everybody else is completely wrong.

But after reading these parables, one fact that should have become clear to you is that the establishment of the kingdom of God wouldn't eliminate evil right away. As Jesus began to teach about His kingdom, He stated plainly that good and bad were going to coexist and compete for a while. People would have to make a choice about which side they would pursue. Some of Jesus' longer parables make the point more specifically.

Read Matthew 13:1-12.
In the Parable of the Sower, what do you think is represented by:

❏ The seed?

❏ The hard soil on the path?

❏ The rocky places?

❏ The shallow soil?

❏ The good soil?

Jesus' disciples didn't understand why Jesus just didn't come out and say what He meant. What did Jesus tell them? (Matthew 13:10-12)

Read Matthew 13:18-23.
Jesus went on to give an explanation for the Parable of the Sower. Does He include any information in His interpretation that you had misinterpreted or missed altogether?

Read Matthew 13:24-30.
A similar parable is found here. This passage is known as the Parable of the Weeds. Who or what do you think Jesus was representing by:

❏ The sower?

❏ The good seed?

❏ The field?

❏ The weeds?

❏ The enemy?

After Jesus told the Parable of the Weeds, His disciples were again confused. Jesus had told several parables, but they were especially interested in what this one meant (Matthew 13:36).

Read Matthew 13:37-43.
How far was your own explanation from Jesus' interpretation?

Your Money Where Your Mouth Is

Read Matthew 21:28-32.
In addition to the parables that illustrated the ongoing struggle between good and evil, Jesus also told parables to caution us to make sure our actions matched our intentions. A lot of people say they want to oppose evil and do good, but their actions don't show it. What parable did Jesus tell to illustrate this point? (Matthew 21:28-30)

Jesus was talking to the chief priests and elders of the temple when He told the previous parable (Matthew 21:23). After He finished the parable, how did He interpret it for them? (Matthew 21:31-32)

Good intentions are important. Good actions are even better than good intentions. But we can still run into problems if we try to judge other people's actions instead of letting Jesus do so. In His Sermon on the Mount, Jesus had warned of the dangers of judging others. Since we will never be as informed and qualified as He is, the judging is best left up to Him.

Read Matthew 20:1-16.
Jesus used this parable to illustrate the difference between His standards and ours. What was the arrangement the landowner made with the first workers he hired? (Matthew 20:1-2)

[NOTE: The word *denarius* used in some Bible translations was the average daily wage during this time.]

When the landowner went to find additional workers, it was "about the third hour," or around 9 A.M. What arrangement did he make with these workers? (Matthew 20:3-4)

The landowner made additional recruiting trips at the sixth hour (noon), the ninth hour (3 P.M.), and the eleventh hour (you guessed it—5 P.M.). How much pay did the people receive who were hired last? (Matthew 20:5-9)

The all-day workers got pretty excited when they saw how much the people received who had only worked for an hour. What happened to cool their excitement? (Matthew 20:10-12)

Do you think they had a valid argument? Explain.

What did the landowner say in defense of his payment structure? (Matthew 20:13-15)

What point was Jesus making? (Matthew 20:16)

Getting Personal — *What do you think about this parable? Was the land-owner within his rights, or was he unfair?*

Better On Time Than Never

As He shows in another couple of parables, Jesus was in no way saying that it's OK to put off making a decision to work for Him.

Read Luke 12:35-48.
What should be our attitude while serving Jesus? (Luke 12:35-40)

What will be the consequences of an improper attitude? (Luke 12:41-48)

Read Matthew 25:6-13.
Another (more familiar) parable also stresses the importance of remaining ready at all times for Jesus' return. Jesus makes His point with a contrast. What two groups of people did He describe, and what was the situation? (Matthew 25:1-5)

What happened to differentiate one group of people from the other? (Matthew 25:6-12)

What did Jesus want us to learn from the parable? (Matthew 25:13)

Getting Personal — *Who are you most like in this parable? Why?*

Read Matthew 22:1-14.
In another parable, Jesus again uses the illustration of a wedding banquet. This one was being given by a king for his son. After everything was all ready, the invited people refused to come (and even mistreated and killed the king's servants). The king retaliated by destroying the people who had

101

rejected him and killed his people. But he still wanted the banquet to go on. So what did he do? (Matthew 22:1-10)

It was customary during this time for the king to provide proper wedding garments for his guests—especially since these people had been taken right off the streets. But one guest apparently didn't feel obliged to wear the appropriate clothing that had been provided for him. What were the consequences of this man's lack of action? (Matthew 22:11-14)

How does this parable relate to proper attitudes and actions?

As you have seen, Jesus had much to say about the kingdom of God in His parables. Through His stories, Jesus revealed many of the "mysteries" of the kingdom. He explained the different ways people respond to spiritual truth. He demonstrated the value of the kingdom of heaven in relation to the other things we value. He illustrated the spiritual conflict between His followers and the devil. He spoke of His eventual (and inevitable) return to earth, which will be accompanied by a separation process where God will reward the faithful and judge those who have refused to put their trust in Him.

The next session will move from the parables into some of the direct teachings of Jesus (many of which are also difficult to comprehend). But don't abandon this session until you've struggled a bit with the parables it contains.

 JOURNEY INWARD

Perhaps the "mysteries" of this session have raised some questions in your mind. If not, you're probably not putting enough thought into your answers. When Jesus first revealed these spiritual "secrets" in His parables, He raised more questions than He answered. And even though Christians have had almost 2,000 years to work on the meaning of those parables, many of Jesus'

words are still mysterious. We still must search for clues and uncover all the evidence we can to try to understand these **spiritual mysteries.**

Start with the information you've just completed. Do you have any questions about the material in this session? If so, write your questions below.

Now expand your thinking to the realm of spirituality/Christianity as a whole. What other questions do you have about God, Jesus, religion, the Bible, and so forth? Write them below.

Of all the questions you listed above, single out the one that you would most like to know the answer to. (Put a √ mark beside it.)

Now, even though you think this session is almost over, you won't be finished until you do a little detective work. The question you've chosen is your mystery, and your assignment is to come up with some clues that will help you solve it. A good detective will begin by checking with all his or her sources. See what you can discover from:

❑ The Bible itself—What familiar passages relate to your question?

❑ A Bible Concordance—What *new* passages can you find to help you?

❑ Bible Commentaries—If your question concerns a specific Bible passage, what do other authorities have to say about it?

❑ Other "detectives"—Where can you find good books to help you with your question? (Church or public libraries? Bookstores?) Who could you discuss your question with who might already have thought through the same issue? (Friends? Pastor? Teacher?)

❏ God Himself—Since God is the Provider of wisdom (James 1:5), what do you need to do in order to maintain a strong relationship with Him as you search for the answer to your question? (Pray? Spend time alone with Him?)

Even if you don't completely solve your mystery, you'll probably uncover enough good information to help you understand it a lot more clearly. And if you do get it solved, go to work on another mystery on your list. Who knows? Before long you may get so good at this that you can become a consulting detective to help other people answer their questions.

 KEY VERSE

"The knowledge of the secrets of the kingdom of heaven has been given to you . . . whoever has will be given more, and he will have an abundance. Whoever does not have, even what he has will be taken from him" (Matthew 13:11-12).

*How well could you plow if you kept looking
behind you instead of looking forward?*

9

YOU CAN'T PLOW STRAIGHT
IF YOU'RE LOOKING BEHIND YOU

(Jesus: His Teachings)

Sarah and Nicole had just finished their daily workout. After determining last fall to try to get in shape by spring, they faithfully exercised every day (almost) throughout the winter. They found a couple of exercise videos they liked, and started a regular routine. By the first warm days in spring, they were feeling (and looking) pretty good. And since they saw such good results from their physical discipline, Sarah had a brainstorm.

"We should make a video for spiritual exercise, since these physical workouts are so successful."

Nicole winced. "I can see it now: 'Get Spiritual with Sarah.' You would be up in front of a bunch of people saying, 'Now let's bend those knees in prayer. Ten more minutes. . . nine more. . . .'"

"No, nothing like that."

But Nicole wouldn't give up. "Work those arms in outreach. . . ."

"No, no, no."

"Broaden your shoulders by bearing one another's burdens. . . ."

"Stop it, Nicole."

"Tighten those sagging facial muscles by smiling. . . ."

"I'm not talking about adapting regular exercises for Christians," Sarah said. "I just think if people can benefit so much from regular physical workouts, why wouldn't they benefit even more from a daily *spiritual* workout?"

"I don't know how you could do anything on video. . . or in groups. It's kind of a personal thing."

"I guess you're right. It just seems that more people could stand to be reminded to work a little harder at their spiritual development."

"I still like the exercise idea. 'Pump up those finger muscles by extensive Bible page-turning. Exercise your eyeballs with intensive reading.'"

Sarah shrieked, "Forget it. Just forget it." Then she threw a pillow at Nicole for some additional vigorous exercise.

Sarah's idea isn't a bad one. At least, her observations are correct. People who are into running, weight-lifting, or many other sports are "fanatics" when it comes to commitment—and they're proud of it. Yet those same people often have trouble maintaining a 10-minute daily devotional. You will see in this session that a lack of discipline when it comes to spiritual things can have severe consequences.

 JOURNEY ONWARD

Throughout this book you've been following the life of Jesus. You've seen His relationships, based on compassion rather than selfishness. You've seen His power to heal the sick, forgive sins, cast out demons, control nature, and so forth. You've heard His explanation to many of the mysteries of the kingdom of God. Large crowds of people followed Him everywhere He went. Now here's a question for you: What happened?

When Jesus was on trial and about to be crucified, where were these large groups of people? Were the people who were yelling, "Crucify Him," the same ones who had followed Him as disciples at one time? Why, all of a sudden, would the crowd want a common thief released from custody rather than Jesus, who had done only good things for them?

You probably have your own answer(s) to those questions. But part of the reason was probably the fact that Jesus taught some things that many of the people didn't understand. And since they didn't try to "exercise" or "stretch" their spiritual thinking, they willfully allowed Jesus to be killed.

Many of Jesus' teachings dealt with who He is. Look up each of the following passages to discover who or what Jesus said He was. Then describe why Jesus used that description of Himself. (You may recognize some of these descriptions from previous sessions.)

REFERENCE	DESCRIPTION OF JESUS	WHY DESCRIPTION IS APPROPRIATE
Matthew 9:14-15		
Matthew 12:1-14 (especially v. 8)		
John 6:35-51		
John 10:1-21 (especially v. 11)		
John 10:22-42 (especially v. 30)		

Getting Personal—*Which of the above descriptions best fits your own perception of Jesus?*

As you read through these passages, did you notice the reactions of the people to these statements of Jesus? Some believed, sure, but others didn't react so positively. They accused Him of being crazy and demon-possessed (John 10:20). They picked up rocks to stone Him (John 10:31). They tried to seize Him (John 10:39). They plotted to kill Him (Matthew 12:14).

Remember that we're not talking about gang members here. A lot of these people were Pharisees. Synagogue officials. Religious leaders. People who knew much of the Old Testament Scripture by heart and were actually looking for a Savior to come. But as knowledgeable as these people were, they sure weren't all that smart. They couldn't (or wouldn't) stretch their thinking to seriously try to understand the things Jesus was saying.

Read John 6:53-66.

There was another kind of reaction to Jesus' teachings—not so violent, but equally severe for those involved. You've just read John 6:35-51 where Jesus was describing Himself as the Bread of Life. If you had read a little farther, you would have discovered that the crowd couldn't understand Jesus' references to "eat the flesh of the Son of man and drink His blood" (John 6:53). How did many of the people respond to these statements? (John 6:60-66)

If the people had stuck around for a while, and maybe asked some questions, they would have soon discovered that Jesus wasn't promoting cannibalism. Rather, He was stating (very strongly) that He is the source of life. He later gave His disciples symbols of His body and blood at the Last Supper (Luke 22:19-20). But whole crowds of people gave up on Jesus much too soon because they weren't willing to struggle a little bit with what He was saying.

Jesus could have spent His time being more "tactful" and playing up to the egos of the Pharisees. But He refused to water down His message. He knew what people were thinking and how willing (or resistant) they were to hear what He had to say. And since the Pharisees refused to exercise any faith toward Him, Jesus refused to overlook their attitudes just because they were religious leaders. Whenever they tried to twist what He was saying, He could put the pressure right back on them.

Read Matthew 15:1-20.

For example, the Pharisees put much emphasis on being "clean" (pure before God). But they had lost out on the true definition of cleanliness. In one instance, they tried to make a big deal about the fact that Jesus' disciples didn't always wash their hands before eating (Matthew 15:1-2). Jesus first chided the Pharisees for bogging down God's clear instructions with a lot of nitpicky rules of their own (Matthew 15:3-6). Then what did Jesus tell the Pharisees? (Matthew 15:7-9)

Getting Personal — *In what areas do you tend to place too much emphasis on tradition or rules? What can you do to change that tendency?*

According to Jesus, what makes people "unclean"? (Matthew 15:10-20)

Read Matthew 12:38-42; 16:1-4.
On other occasions, the Pharisees asked to see a miraculous sign from heaven (as if Jesus hadn't yet done anything noteworthy). How did Jesus respond to these requests?

Getting Personal — *Do external or supernatural signs play a dramatic part in your faith?*

Read Matthew 16:5-12.
Jesus then warned His disciples to "be on your guard against the yeast of the Pharisees and Sadducees." (The Sadducees were another Jewish party similar to the Pharisees, but who were a little less conservative in their thinking and a little more political in their approach to life.) What did Jesus mean?

Read Matthew 12:22-37.
The Pharisees didn't rely only on open debate to oppose Jesus. They did whatever they could to cast doubts on His power and His good intentions. Once Jesus healed a man who couldn't talk, couldn't see, and was demon-possessed. The people who saw it were amazed and began to realize that Jesus might be "the Son of David" (which was one of their titles for the Messiah). How did the Pharisees explain the miracle in a way to keep Jesus (and God) from receiving credit for it? (Matthew 12:22-24)

How did Jesus explain that the accusations of the Pharisees didn't make any sense? (Matthew 12:25-28)

Jesus went on to describe how dangerous was the attitude of the Pharisees. What sin did Jesus say would not be forgiven? (Matthew 12:30-32)

How important are the words we use? Why? (Matthew 12:34-37)

Getting Personal — *How do you feel about being judged according to your words?*

Read Luke 16:10-15.
What was another teaching of Jesus that the Pharisees tried to laugh off? Why? (Luke 16:10-15)

It should again be noted that Jesus was addressing the Pharisees in general. Just because a person happened to be a Pharisee didn't automatically make him a selfish and proud opponent of Jesus. Some of the Pharisees were good men, but many others weren't.

Jesus had a lot to say, whether or not the Pharisees were hanging around and trying to provoke Him. He regularly challenged His disciples to flex their spiritual muscles and comprehend the things He was trying to teach them. What did He want them to learn about the following topics?

❑ Greatness (Matthew 18:1-4)

❑ Settling disagreements (Matthew 18:15-20)

❑ The seriousness of causing someone else to sin (Mark 9:42-50)

❑ Divorce (Mark 10:1-12)

❑ John the Baptist (Luke 7:24-35)

❑ Prayer (Luke 11:1-13)

❑ Life after death (Luke 16:19-31)

❑ His (Jesus') relationship with God (John 5:19-23)

Read Matthew 16:13-23.
And though the disciples were a little slow to learn, eventually some of Jesus' teaching did begin to sink in. What was one thing Peter came to realize that caused Jesus to compliment him?

At this time, Jesus noted that a better name for Simon would be Peter (which means *rock*). But Jesus had seen Peter's potential from the beginning. (See John 1:42.) Why do you think Jesus chose this time to emphasize Simon Peter's name change?

But soon afterward, when Jesus began to predict His death, Peter didn't come off looking so good. What did Peter say that caused Jesus to scold him? (Matthew 16:21-23)

Counting the Cost
Read Luke 13:2-30.
Jesus knew it wasn't easy for people to follow Him faithfully. You've seen before that some people who committed to believe in Jesus could experience negative consequences (like the blind man in John 9 who got kicked out of the synagogue and lost the friendship of several of his neighbors and family members). What challenge did Jesus offer His listeners when they began to wonder how many people would actually be saved?

Read Matthew 20:20-28.
Jesus also continued to challenge them to try to live by a different standard than the rest of the world. One time the mother of disciples James and John asked Jesus for a special favor. What did she want? (Matthew 20:20-22)

What did Jesus tell her? (Matthew 20:23)

When the rest of the disciples got a little aggravated with James and John, what did Jesus tell them? (Matthew 20:24-28)

Getting Personal — *How would you have felt if you were James or John? Their mother? One of the other disciples?*

Read Luke 9:57-61.
Sometimes Jesus may even have sounded cruel when He told people what they must do to be one of His followers. In Jesus' discussions with others, what were some of the reasons that came up for not following Him?

Jesus realized that people would always be able to find a reason not to follow Him. And some of their reasons would be very good ones. But following Jesus is something that must take first priority in our lives if we want everything else to fall into place.

Read Luke 14:25-27.
You know that Jesus has taught us to love even our enemies. So what do you think He means here when He says we should hate everyone in our families before we can be His disciple?

Getting Personal — *What has it cost you to follow Jesus?*

Read Luke 9:62.
Jesus used another example to make the point in this verse. Imagine you're a farmer during Jesus' time in history. You hitch your plow to your mule and go out to plow your field. The soil is dry and hard, and it's difficult to maintain a straight furrow. How well do you think you'd do if you kept looking behind you instead of looking forward?

Jesus wasn't promoting hatred among family members. He wasn't saying it was a bad thing to want to bury dead relatives or to want a place to stay at night. But He made it clear that the most important thing in the life of a disciple should be his or her relationship with Him. He was and is the source of all life.

Jesus' teachings were extremely hard for His followers to understand. Many of them still are. But the quality of our lives and futures may well depend on how hard we try to understand and believe everything He taught. No amount of struggle or discomfort now could ever compare to the reward He will give those who determine to follow Him—no matter what.

JOURNEY INWARD

The first step in understanding many of the hard teachings of Jesus is actually rather easy. In the last session, you played detective and learned to seek out clues and follow sources. Now it's just a matter of actually doing it. So to close this session, give yourself a **spiritual workout.**

When you begin to "stretch" yourself physically, the first week or so is tough. Your strenuous, sweaty workouts can be inconvenient and uncomfortable at first (especially if you're not used to them). But in the long run, the results will be good health, a stronger body, an emotional uplift, and satisfaction with your ability to discipline yourself. The secret is to get through the initial discomfort enough times to become accustomed to the little bit of extra effort.

It's important to "stretch" yourself spiritually as well as physically. When you decide to work a little harder on your spiritual development, you may experience a little awkwardness. But the only way to benefit from the process is to stick with it until it becomes comfortable to you. The first thing to do is evaluate your current level of spiritual development. How much time do you spend daily (on an average) in each of the following activities:

	HOURS	MINUTES	SECONDS
Personal Prayer:			
Praise to God			
Thanksgiving			
Confession			
Requests for yourself			
Requests for others			
Other: _____			
Prayer with others			
Personal Bible study			
Scripture memory			
Service activities			
Group activities			
Bible studies			
Prayer meetings			
Other: _____			

After making the evaluation of your current status, you should try to gradually increase the amount of energy you are presently exerting. (Like physical exercise, you don't want to do too much too soon or your plan can backfire.)

First check to see if there are any areas on the previous list that you should be involved in, but aren't. Then see if you should be devoting more time to one or more of the activities. Finally, put together your plan for a "Personal Spiritual Workout" by completing the following pledges.

This week I will begin my spiritual development by:

Next week I will:

At some later point I want to start:

Don't be too discouraged if you commit to something and then fizzle out. It's not easy to get started and keep going. Just rethink your program and start over again . . . and again and again if necessary. Yes, it's hard to discipline yourself to stick to good spiritual habits and continue to increase your commitment. But much of what Jesus wants you to understand is also hard. So hang in there. As soon as you start putting together the pieces of some of these complicated spiritual principles, you'll be glad you made the effort. So will Jesus.

 KEY VERSE

"Anyone who loves his father or mother more than Me is not worthy of Me; anyone who loves his son or daughter more than Me is not worthy of Me; and anyone who does not take his cross and follow Me is not worthy of Me. Whoever finds his life will lose it, and whoever loses his life for My sake will find it" (Matthew 10:37-39).

It would be great to have six hands when deadlines approach!

10

COUNTDOWN!

(Jesus: His Last Days)

February 10
Dear Diary,
Today Professor Southern gave me an assignment for the paper he's presenting at the National Conference of American History Professors. He wants 20 pages on a topic from American history by May 15. Once he receives all the assigned reports, he'll decide which person will be his research assistant. On a more optimistic note, I went to the mall today and bought a red sweater. Hope John likes it. . . .

March 10
Dear Diary,
Mr. Southern reminded me today about my research paper. Eleanor is doing "The Political Significance of the Bull Moose Party and Its Economic Ramifications on the Nation's Businesses." Guess that's one topic I can rule out for myself. (Ha Ha!) Seriously, I have to decide on a topic soon. By the way, every time I wear my new sweater, John says how much he likes it. So I went out and got a yellow one. . . .

March 28
Dear Diary,
My life is a wreck. John started going out with Lisa. Maybe I'll do the St. Valentines Day Massacre for my paper. And I spilled grape juice on my yellow sweater, so it's too late to take it back. . . .

April 15
Dear Diary,
I sent my tax forms in today. Don't know why I didn't do it sooner. It's not like me to put things off. I'm getting some money back and I already know how I'm going to spend it. Now I'd better get serious about my paper. I need this research job. And good news—Lisa broke up with John.

April 28
Diary,
Gotta keep it short tonight. I am not leaving my room till I decide on a topic! P.S.—John's really being nice to me these days.

April 30
Dear Diary,
I've finally decided. It's either going to be, "The Spirit of 1776: Where Is It Today?" or "William Howard Taft: Pound for Pound the Best President We Ever Had." Gotta go. John's taking me bowling.

May 1
Dear Diary,
My mind's made up. My paper will be titled: "Millard Fillmore: Our Forgotten Hero." I'm off to the library now. I've got two whole weeks. No problem. How much could have happened during Millard Fillmore's administration, anyway?

May 2
Dear Diary,
I'm in trouble now. I thought Millard Fillmore would be a breeze, but Mr. Southern says he needs information on the world events, literature, mood of the country, and everything else that happened during his presidency. That means I have to know about Daniel Webster, his Secretary of State. Harriet Beecher Stowe's *Uncle Tom's Cabin* kept the slavery issue on everyone's mind. The first successful airship was launched. School attendance became mandatory for the first time. Active writers included Nathanael Hawthorne, Herman Melville, Ralph Waldo Emerson, Henry Wadsworth Longfellow, and Charles Dickens. It's going to take me years to do this paper!

May 16
Dear Diary,
I finally get to write you again. After two weeks of intensive cramming, I know more about Millard Fillmore than anyone would ever want to. I was even able to

work in Amelia Bloomer's new fashion trend and her contribution to women's suffrage. I feel good about my paper. I'm pretty sure I'll get the job, but I had to give up a lot during these past two weeks. No shopping. No TV. And no John. But knowing I did a good job makes the temporary inconvenience seem worth it. Oops. The phone's ringing. I wonder if it could be. . . .

You've probably never found yourself in a situation similar to this one. No doubt you always do work assignments as soon as they're given to you, leaving lots of spare time to bootleg other activities. But believe it or not, many people put off their work, home maintenance, and other projects until the last minute.

It's kind of fun to sit back and watch people as deadlines approach for them. As the "day of reckoning" gets nearer, more and more of their thoughts and energies begin to focus on that one crucial project. When they finally come to the realization that their time is about up, they put all or most of their effort into making sure they do what needs to get done the most. For example, how many times have you seen a family leaving for vacation, rushing around like crazy people to do "last minute" things, though they knew months before exactly when they would be leaving?

 JOURNEY ONWARD

As you've been working your way through the Gospels and examining the life of Jesus, you can probably recall several times when Jesus spoke of His death. He knew who was going to betray Him (John 6:70-71), how He would die (John 3:14-15), and how long He would be in the tomb (Matthew 12:40). Such knowledge might be more than most of us could handle. We know that Jesus never deviated from His mission to reach the world with the story (and example) of God's love, yet we might do well to pay special attention to Jesus' words and actions during His last days. Knowing that He only had a short time left, these are the instructions and topics that Jesus chose to deal with.

Read Matthew 20:17-19.
As the end grew nearer for Jesus, He became more specific as He spoke with His disciples. What did He tell them to try to prepare them for what was to come?

Read Matthew 17:1-13.
Jesus had been revealing His power to the disciples a little at a time. After they had seen many of His miracles, Jesus promised that "some who are standing here will not taste death before they see the Son of man coming in His kingdom" (Matthew 16:28). Six days later, Jesus allowed some of the disciples to see something they hadn't seen before. Who was present? (Matthew 17:1)

What did these disciples see? (Matthew 17:2-3)

Peter seemed to think that Jesus was in pretty good company, and was going to do something that would "honor" Him in the same way the other two visitors would be honored. But before Peter could even get the suggestion out of his mouth, what happened? (Matthew 17:4-5)

What request did Jesus make of His disciples? (Matthew 17:6-9)

When the disciples reminded Jesus that Elijah was prophesied to return before the Messiah came (Malachi 4:5), what did Jesus tell them? (Matthew 17:10-13)

Getting Personal — *When was the last time you had a "Mountaintop experience"? What was its impact on your life?*

Read Matthew 21:1-11.
At this point in Jesus' ministry, the reaction toward Him was very much mixed. You may remember from Session 6 that after Jesus raised Lazarus from the dead, a group of disgruntled religious leaders seriously began to

look for a way to arrest and/or kill Him (John 11:45-57). At that time they thought that perhaps they could find Him at the Feast of the Passover. And sure enough, that's where Jesus was going. But before He got to Jerusalem, what arrangements did He make? (Matthew 21:1-5)

What kind of reception did Jesus get as He went riding into Jerusalem? (Matthew 21:6-11)

Getting Personal—*How would you have greeted Jesus as He entered Jerusalem?*

Read Luke 19:37-44.
It's apparent that Jesus' critics weren't the only ones looking for Him, but they were among the crowd. What did they want Jesus to do? (Luke 19:37-39)

What was Jesus' response? (Luke 19:40)

What did Jesus do when He saw the city of Jerusalem? Why? (Luke 19:41-44)

Read Mark 11:11-26.
Jesus knew He would die less than a week after this "triumphant" entrance into Jerusalem, but He went about His daily routine. After entering the city and visiting the temple, it was late. So Jesus and His disciples went to the nearby city of Bethany (Mark 11:11). As they returned to Jerusalem the next morning, what happened? (Mark 11:12-14)

When Jesus and the disciples reached Jerusalem, Jesus did something He had done once before (early in His ministry). What did He do? (Mark 11:15-18; see also John 2:13-16.)

Again, Jesus spent the night in Bethany and returned to Jerusalem the next day. What was significant about His trip into the city that next morning? (Mark 11:20-21)

It would be out of character for Jesus to walk around randomly smiting foliage that wouldn't provide Him with food. More likely, His action was a symbolic attempt to teach His disciples something. What you may not know is that by the time fig trees get leafy, they should also have a number of edible buds. A tree without these buds would not bear figs later on in the year. What do you think Jesus was trying to symbolize by showing His displeasure with something that showed outward signs of maturity, but actually wasn't fruitful at all?

What did Jesus promise His disciples immediately after this incident? (Mark 11:22-26)

Trick Questions
Read Luke 20:2-8.
As Jesus went through His last week before His crucifixion, the religious leaders were trying their hardest to find some serious offense for which He could be arrested. One of their tricks was to try to get Him to say something that they could twist around and use against Him. One direct question they asked Him was, "Who gave You this authority?" (Luke 20:2) By this they were probably referring to His clearing out the temple.

This was one of those questions that, when asked with the intent only to cause trouble, probably could never be answered satisfactorily. Suppose Jesus had publicly stated that He had been dropped out of heaven by God (who, by the way, happened to be His Father) to save the world from the penalty of its sin. The religious leaders would have spent months cross-examining Him and trying to pick apart everything He said. So what did Jesus do to keep from giving the religious leaders the embarrassing scene they were looking for? (Luke 20:3-8)

Read Matthew 22:15-22.
Another attempt to trip Jesus up was in the area of paying taxes. Knowing how many of the people hated to be under Roman rule, what was the trick question the Pharisees asked Jesus? (Matthew 22:15-17)

How did Jesus respond? (Matthew 22:18-22)

Getting Personal — *After reading this passage, how do you feel about paying taxes?*

More of Jesus' conversation with the Pharisees and religious leaders is found in Matthew 22:23–23:39 and Luke 11:37-54. He says a lot of harsh things about these people who were using religion for their own benefit. You should read through these sections sometime when you have time to think about them for a while, and perhaps pull out some commentaries to help explain more of the subtleties of what Jesus was saying. But one statement is noteworthy at this point.

Read Matthew 22:34-40.
When Jesus was asked what was the most important commandment in Scripture, what did He say?

After Jesus left the temple, the disciples found Him by Himself and began to quiz Him about His return to earth and the signs of the end of the age. Jesus gave them plenty to look for and think about.

Skim Matthew 24.
List the signs and events that will take place in connection with the end of the world as we know it. (You may also want to read Luke 17:20-37.)

Read Matthew 25:31-46.
Jesus also explained how He would determine who would receive the inheritance of God and who would receive eternal punishment. How would He separate the righteous people from the wicked?

Read Matthew 26:1-5.
After explaining this to His disciples, Jesus again reminded them that He would die soon. And what were the religious leaders up to at this time?

Read John 12:2-8.
Yet in Bethany, where Jesus was staying, He was still receiving honor. In the first place, He had been invited to dinner by a man called Simon the Leper (Matthew 26:6). It seems logical that perhaps Simon had been healed of his leprosy by Jesus. Also at this dinner were Mary, Martha, and Lazarus (John 12:2-3). What did Mary do at the dinner to honor Jesus? (John 12:3)

How did Judas Iscariot react to Mary's action? Why? (John 12:4-6)

How did Jesus react to Mary's action? (John 12:7-8)

[This account is similar to the one in Luke 7:36-50 that you read in Session 7. But enough of the facts are different (the time of the event, the location, the status of the host, etc.) to indicate that there were two separate anointings of Jesus. Mary's actions took place just a couple of days before Jesus died.]

Read John 12:23-44.
On another occasion during this final week, Jesus again predicted His death. To what did He compare it? (John 12:23-26)

How could the disciples be sure of what Jesus was saying? (John 12:27-33)

What challenge did Jesus offer His listeners? (John 12:34-36)

And even though Jesus was spending His final week in an intensive schedule of debating the Pharisees, teaching the disciples, and preparing to be killed, He didn't overlook the big "little" things that were important. What did Jesus see that was worth calling His disciples together to discuss, and why do you think this action was so important to Jesus? (Mark 12:41-44)

Read Matthew 26:14-16; Luke 22:1-6.
You might assume that anyone who had observed all the things the disciples had seen couldn't be influenced by anyone or anything to take a stand against Jesus. But a commitment to Jesus has to be a person's choice; it's never automatic. Consequently, one of the disciples was vulnerable to the temptation of Satan to make some money by betraying Jesus. You know that the disciple was Judas. What specific arrangement did he make with the religious leaders?

From this point, the events of Jesus' crucifixion and resurrection went speeding by rapidly. But before we move on to those topics, we should stop now for a little reflection of our own.

 JOURNEY INWARD

This session has focused on the assumption that Jesus, since He had only a little bit of time left with His friends, must have selected His teachings with care. This was no time for discussions that really didn't have that much to do with the kingdom of heaven. And it would be helpful for you to review everything you've studied in this session and make those principles important to yourself as well. But to close this session, we want to look at a subject that's quite different from what we've been examining—**rejection.**

Everybody hates rejection. Being rejected means that a person isn't considered good enough, rich enough, smart enough, talented enough, or whatever. And we're often quick to get depressed and give up on ourselves when we're rejected. Yet as you've seen in this session, Jesus knew He was going to be rejected. People were going to make fun of Him. Some of His closest friends would deny and betray Him. He would be falsely arrested, physically abused, spat upon, and hated. And yes, He was eventually going to be killed—for no good reason.

Yet even though Jesus was always aware of this impending, ultimate rejection, do you notice any changes in His lifestyle? Do you notice Him taking out His feelings on anyone else? Do you see Him sulking? Do you observe Him compromising His standards to get people to like Him more? Jesus had more reason than anyone who has ever lived to be upset by rejection. He was God in human form, sinless and perfect. And His rejection was more undeserved than anything we will ever face. But He went on doing what He knew He should be doing, and He didn't let rejection slow Him down.

To help you evaluate how much you are affected by rejection, finish the incomplete sentences that follow.

(1) I really hate it when people don't appreciate the fact that I've....

(2) Rejection hurts most when it comes from. . . .

(3) When I begin to feel rejected, I. . . .

(4) When I face major rejection, I. . . .

(5) To get over my rejection, I usually. . . .

(6) If I could avoid rejection for good, I'd be willing to. . . .

After you complete your sentences, spend some time in prayer and ask Jesus for patience to deal with rejection more like He did. Don't ask to avoid all types of rejection, because rejection is something that good Christians are going to face, like it or not. (See the **Key Verse** at the end of this chapter.)

Then think back on how Jesus spent His last days. Recall how He kept on doing all the things that were important, even though He knew He would very soon face the total rejection of death on a cross. And finally, design your own Plan for Facing Rejection. Come up with at least three things you will do the next time you are insulted, forgotten about, ignored, betrayed, etc. And don't just write your Plan and forget about it. Write it and use it! If you learn to repel rejection now, there's probably nothing that can prevent you from being successful in life.

MY PLAN FOR FACING REJECTION

KEY VERSE

"If the world hates you, keep in mind that it hated Me first. If you belonged to the world, it would love you as its own. As it is, you do not belong to the world, but I have chosen you out of the world. That is why the world hates you" (John 15:18-19).

Jesus knew when His death would take place.
Suppose you only had a month to live. How would you respond?

11

CROSS PURPOSES

(Jesus: His Crucifixion)

Suppose you knew you had only a month to live. Imagine that your health will not be impaired in any way and that your friends and family have taken up a collection to let you do anything and everything you want to do. Money is no object. How would you focus your attention in each of the following areas?

PEOPLE—Who would you spend your time with? How long would you spend with each person/group?

PLACES—Where would you spend your last month? What places would you want to visit? How long would you spend in each place?

ACTIVITIES—How would you want to spend your time? Would you go about your normal routine? Take up new and exotic hobbies? Write a will?

SPIRITUAL ACTIVITIES—Would you spend any extra time with God? Ask Him for anything special? Look up Bible passages on heaven/eternity?

Wouldn't it be kind of eerie to know exactly when you were going to die? As insecure as you might feel because you know you're eventually going to die "someday," it would be even more frightening to have a date marked on your calendar. With every sunrise you would be reminded that you were one day closer to that date. But on the other hand, you might not be so likely to waste time or hold grudges if you knew each day was precious.

Jesus was in the unusual position of knowing when, where, and how He was going to die. In the last session you saw how He spent His last days—just going about His usual business. But in this session, you're going to see exactly what He had envisioned since He began His public ministry. Jesus had come to earth to die, and perhaps no one but He knew how severe (and undeserved) His death would be. As you work through this session, keep in mind what kind of person it would take to go through what Jesus experienced without displaying some kind of hatred or retaliation.

 JOURNEY ONWARD

Read Mark 14:12-25.

At the end of the last session, you read of Judas' agreement with the Jewish religious leaders to betray Jesus. Of course, Jesus had known that this was coming for a long while. But He didn't show any signs of panic as He planned for what would be His last meal with His disciples. This was a special meal for a lot of people, because it was the annual celebration of the Passover (Exodus 12). What arrangements did the disciples make in order to eat the Passover meal? (Mark 14:12-16)

What was one of the things that Jesus did during the Last Supper? (Mark 14:22-25)

Read Matthew 26:20-25; John 13:21-30.

One of the topics of conversation at the Last Supper was Jesus' betrayal. When Jesus announced that one of His disciples would betray Him, what was the response?

Read Luke 22:24-30.
Another topic of discussion was greatness. What did Jesus tell the disciples to do if they wanted to be great?

Read John 13:1-17.
How did Jesus demonstrate what He had just taught about greatness? (John 13:1-5)

Getting Personal — *When you first became a Christian, who demonstrated a servant attitude toward you? Have you ever thanked that person?*

How did Peter respond to this action, and why do you think he did so? (John 13:6-9)

What did Jesus want His disciples to learn? (John 13:10-17)

Read Luke 22:35-38.
But even though Jesus wanted His disciples to serve others, He also wanted to prepare them for the harsh realities of the world. What instructions did He give them?

Read Matthew 26:31-35.
Before the supper was over, Jesus passed along what prediction for Peter?

Jesus didn't want His death to leave His disciples confused and disoriented. At this point He tried to assure the disciples that everything would be OK. What did He tell them about each of the following areas:

❑ The future (John 14:1-4)

❑ The way to find God (John 14:5-14)

❑ The Holy Spirit (John 14:15-31)

❑ A disciple's relationship with Jesus (John 15:1-17)

❑ A disciple's relationship with the world (John 15:18–16:4)

In the Garden
Read Matthew 26:36-39.
After supper, Jesus and the disciples went to a garden called Gethsemane. After Jesus entered the garden, what request did He make of His disciples?

Read John 17:1-26.
This passage contains a portion of Jesus' prayer while He was in Gethsemane. Why did Jesus pray for Himself? (John 17:1-5)

Why did Jesus pray for His disciples? (John 17:6-19)

Who else did Jesus pray for in the garden that night? (John 17:20-26)

Read Luke 22:39-44.
How intensely did Jesus pray?

Read Matthew 26:40-50.
While Jesus was pouring His heart out to God the Father, what were the disciples (the same disciples who had just promised to die for Him) doing? (Matthew 26:40-44)

After Jesus' third prayer, what happened? (Matthew 26:45-50)

Read John 18:1-11; Mark 14:50.
How did the disciples respond to this sudden invasion of their privacy?

Getting Personal — *Do you ever fall asleep when praying? Who would you want to "watch and pray" with you if you were facing a Gethsemane situation?*

Read Luke 22:49-51.
Do you think being arrested had affected Jesus' basic character?

Read Matthew 26:52-54.
Did Jesus have any options rather than to submit to the Jewish authorities?

Jesus was taken to stand trial before the Jewish high priest and the council (called the "Sanhedrin"). Peter followed secretly and waited in the outer courtyard of the high priest (Matthew 26:57-58). At first no one could find a legal reason to hold Jesus. There was no real evidence, of course, but these guys couldn't even get two people to agree on false evidence. (No one could be convicted on the testimony of fewer than two people.) Finally, two accusers remembered something Jesus had said about the temple. They testified that Jesus had stated that He could destroy the temple and rebuild· it in three days.

Read John 2:18-22.
What had Jesus really said, and what had He meant?

Read Matthew 26:62-75.
Eventually, on what charge did the Jews convict Jesus? (Matthew 26:62-65)

How was He treated by the Jewish council? (Matthew 26:66-68)

As the trial was going on inside, Peter was still outside in the courtyard. While he was there, what happened that caused him some emotional distress? (Matthew 26:69-75)

Getting Personal — *Have you ever felt like Peter must have felt? What brought you back to reality?*

Read Luke 22:60-61.
What made this a particularly painful experience for Peter?

Read Matthew 27:1-10.
Peter wasn't the only one who felt bad about what had happened. Who else

was remorseful, and what did this person do?

Before Pilate
Read John 18:28-38.
Jesus had been sentenced to death by the Jewish Sanhedrin. But since they were under the authority of the Roman government, they lacked the power to enforce a death sentence. So Jesus was taken before the Roman governor, Pilate. What did Pilate think about Jesus?

Read Luke 23:6-12.
Then Pilate discovered what he thought was a loophole. Since Jesus was originally from Galilee, that put Him in the jurisdiction of Herod the "tetrarch" (the ruler of one fourth of a large area). Herod was commonly referred to as king of the area in which Galilee was located. And Herod was in Jerusalem for Passover, so Pilate sent Jesus to him. What interest did Herod have in Jesus?

Read Matthew 27:19.
Since Jesus failed to amuse Herod, He was sent back to Pilate. And Pilate still didn't want to convict Jesus. What might have been in the back of Pilate's mind as he judged the case of the People vs. Jesus of Nazareth?

Read Mark 15:6-14.
Pilate came up with a second loophole to keep from having to sentence Jesus to death. What offer did he make?

Read John 19:1-16.
Pilate later tried still another compromise to satisfy the crowd. What did he do? (John 19:1-5)

But the people wouldn't hear of releasing Jesus. Pilate debated with them for a while, but what did the people say to finally convince him to have Jesus killed? (John 19:6-16, especially v. 12)

Read Matthew 27:24-31.
What did Pilate do before sentencing Jesus? Why? (Matthew 27:24-25)

What had happened to Jesus by this time? (Matthew 27:27-31)

Read Luke 23:26-32.
In the Roman Empire, not much time passed between the order to have someone executed and the actual sentence. In most cases there were no courts of appeals, no conniving lawyers to stall the proceedings, and no phone calls from the governor with last-minute pardons. Jesus was given a cross to carry to His place of execution (John 19:17) — a location called "the Place of the Skull" (also called *Golgotha* [in Aramaic] or *Calvary* [from the Latin *calvaria*]). But in Jesus' weakened condition, He was unable to support the weight of the heavy cross. What arrangements were made for Him at that point? (Luke 23:26)

What observation did Jesus make to those who were mourning for Him? (Luke 23:27-31)

Who else was in this processional? (Luke 23:32)

When they got to Golgotha, Jesus and the two thieves were crucified. This type of death was devised by the Romans for criminals, slaves, and the worst offenders of the law who weren't Roman citizens. The victim was stripped, nailed to a wooden cross (with wrought-iron nails through the wrists and heel bones), and raised for people to see. It was an excruciatingly painful and humiliating way to die.

Getting Personal — *When you think of the worst ways to die, where does crucifixion rank? What impresses you about the way Jesus died?*

Read John 19:19-22.
Even though Pilate had given in to the wishes of the people, he still seemed to have an admiration for Jesus. What did he do to suggest that he didn't exactly dismiss Jesus as a lunatic?

While Jesus was on the cross, what were some of the events that took place?

❏ John 19:23-24

❏ Matthew 27:45

❏ Matthew 27:51

❏ Matthew 27:52-53

Jesus also made several statements from the cross. Familiarize yourself with the conditions of each statement and then write down what Jesus said and the person to whom He was speaking.

	THE PERSON	WHAT JESUS SAID

Luke 23:32-34

Luke 23:39-43

John 19:25-27

Matthew 27:45-50

John 19:28-29

John 19:30

Luke 23:44-46

Read Matthew 27:54-55.
What effect did Jesus' death have on some of those who were present?

Getting Personal — *With whom do you identify most in the story of Jesus' crucifixion? How has Jesus' death impacted your life?*

Read John 19:31-37.
Usually the crucifixion victims would have hung on their crosses for many hours—maybe even a couple of days. But since the Jews were looking forward to celebrating the Passover, they requested that the legs of Jesus and the two thieves be broken. (Breaking the legs would prevent the victims from pushing up and taking a breath, causing them to eventually suffocate in their own body fluids.) But Jesus' legs weren't broken. Why not?

We're going to stop here, even though this may not be a comfortable place to end the session. Whenever Christians discuss the Crucifixion, they are usually quick to jump forward to the Resurrection. But linger a few moments on the image of Jesus on the cross. Then move ahead to the next section.

JOURNEY INWARD

We've come most of the way through this book taking a mostly factual approach to the life of Jesus. It is important to study these passages from an intellectual basis. We need to know what Jesus taught and understand what He meant. We need to familiarize ourselves with Jesus' relationships, parables, miracles, and other teachings. But we will never really come close to comprehending who Jesus is unless we pause to let our hearts and emotions feel what He experienced on the cross. It is the ultimate standard of **God's love.**

Any man who did for us what Jesus did would be considered truly great. But Jesus wasn't just any man. He was God. He had come from heaven for the purpose of bearing the sin of the world. Imagine what it must have taken for the Son of God to leave His Father's side in heaven to come to earth, be born in a manger, live a simple lifestyle with uneducated disciples, and be continually hounded by lepers and various other sick people. Then think of what it must have taken to be convicted and sentenced to death (on a religious charge!), to be beaten, whipped, and spat on, and to ask forgiveness for the men who were shouting out snide remarks and driving nails through His hands and feet. Consider how Jesus must have felt as He bore the sin of the world and was temporarily separated from His usual closeness with God the Father.

When we dare to think about such things, we should come to a different image of Jesus than the one that we sometimes have of a divine being who occasionally wants us to do things we don't want to do. And just to help keep a proper perspective, answer the following questions.

❑ Because of Jesus' death on the cross (way back then), what are some of the personal benefits you can enjoy today? List at least half a dozen.

❑ Do you think you ever face temptations or experience emotions that Jesus hasn't already felt? Explain.

143

❑ Do you think Jesus will ever expect you to do anything that He wasn't willing to do Himself? Explain.

❑ Do you often try to model Jesus' sacrificial kind of love toward others? When you consider the price that might be involved, do you really want to model that kind of love? Be specific.

❑ Do you ever show "love" for others that is more a counterfeit type of love than a genuine reflection of God's love (and that possibly does more harm than good)? Give specific examples.

❑ What are five things that you can do this week to demonstrate God's love better than what you've been doing so far?

You won't be able to sit here for 5 or 10 minutes and then walk away with a full knowledge of the benefits of God's love. But you can gradually begin to focus your thoughts on Jesus' sacrificial love more often. And until God's love is displayed by all your actions, you still have a way to go before you're where you should be. And to be truthful, that goes for all of us.

 KEY VERSE

"With a loud cry, Jesus breathed His last. The curtain of the temple was torn in two from top to bottom. And when the centurion, who stood there in front of Jesus, heard His cry and saw how He died, he said, 'Surely this man was the Son of God!' " (Mark 15:37-39)

Seeds, tiny buds, green leaves, beautiful blooms and flowers, death—all are phases of the life cycle.

12

A SEED IS PLANTED

(Jesus: His Resurrection)

THE SETTING: A DARKENED LABORATORY
The mad doctor cackles and calls for his assistant. "Igor! Come quickly. It is time!"

"Yes, Master. What do you need?"

"The storm is upon us. If we can channel the lightning to the laboratory, my creation will live again!"

A large, still figure lies underneath a heavy tarp. The stolen body and "borrowed" brain wait for the intense electrical shock that will restore life.

••

You've no doubt seen one or more versions of this scene on late-night TV and can take the story from here. As unlikely as it seems, a bolt of lightning will somehow shock the life back into the corpse. The new creature will then stagger around, frighten some innocent people, and will eventually be killed. At least, that's how it always seems to work in the movies.

Thanks to Hollywood, most of us probably have some pretty warped images of resurrection. Perhaps we would do better to look at nature. As the seasons go by, you see tiny buds of life, followed by green leaves and bold, beautiful colors in the blooms and flowers. The green leaves eventually turn into a brilliantly colored panorama. And then, all too soon, they die and drop to the ground. The flowers freeze. And except for a few evergreens, all seems dead and lifeless.

But that "lifeless" stage doesn't last forever. The leaves and flowers die, but the trees and bulbs still contain life. Death is only another phase in their life cycle. The same is true for Christians. Our bodies die, but our spirits continue to live. And someday we will discover that death is not an end, but merely the step we take to get to resurrection and better things.

 JOURNEY ONWARD

You may remember Jesus' words in John 12:24. He used the illustration of a seed to demonstrate what He wanted us to know about life and death. A seed has many good, productive uses. It can be used to provide food for humans. It can be used to provide food for animals (which in turn provide food for humans). It can be used in a third-grader's mosaic craft project. All are profitable uses for a seed. But an even more productive use is to plant that seed and let it "die." In the sacrifice of that single seed, many other seeds will eventually come to life.

Jesus knew all along that His death would be only temporary, but that fact certainly didn't make His dying any easier. Yet you have seen that He faced His death with courage and dignity (and compassion for those around Him). Now we get to the best part of the story.

Read Mark 15:42-45; John 19:38-42.
Jesus' arrest and execution had occurred suddenly, at least as far as His friends and family members knew. No salesmen had called to explain the benefits of life insurance or buying a burial plot in advance. So funeral arrangements suddenly became a concern. Who took care of burying Jesus, and why might this have been a risky thing for this person to do?

Getting Personal — *What is the riskiest thing you have ever done because of Jesus?*

Who helped this person attend to the body of Jesus, and what did he contribute to the burial? (John 19:38-39)

A Seed Is Planted

What was done to make sure that Jesus was dead before these two people got permission to take the body? (Mark 15:44-45)

How was Jesus' body prepared for burial? (John 19:39-42)

Read Matthew 27:59-60.
What was done to secure the burial place?

Getting Personal — *Where do you want to be buried? Why?*

Read Mark 15:47; Luke 23:55-56.
Who else was interested in the burial of Jesus?

You have to wonder where Jesus' regular disciples were during this time. But it's very interesting to see that Jesus had been reaching some of the religious leaders with the things He had said and done. It must have taken an extraordinary amount of courage for these two men to boldly oppose the actions that their peers had taken and to approach the Roman governor for the body of Jesus. While Jesus' regular disciples were taking cover and collecting their wits, these new disciples had an opportunity to take a stand for Jesus.

Read Matthew 27:62-66.
But even though Jesus was dead, other religious leaders feared that their problems might not yet be over. What did these leaders ask Pilate to do?

Read Mark 16:1-3.
After Jesus' death and burial on Friday, not much is said of the next day because it was the Jewish Sabbath. It was improper to do anything "unclean" on that day (such as touching a dead body, even to prepare it for burial). So some of the women who had traveled with Jesus went very early on Sunday morning to anoint His body with spices. And they were concerned about something. What were they trying to figure out?

Missing Person
Read Luke 24:1-3.
When they got to the tomb, they discovered that their problem had already been solved. But what bigger problem did they face?

Getting Personal — *How would you feel if you went to visit a friend's grave and found his/her headstone missing?*

Read Mark 16:5-8.
Apparently, Mary Magdalene went running back to get the disciples (John 20:1-2) while the other women remained. While she was gone, what did the other women discover?

Why do you think the angel singled out Peter (in Mark 16:7) from the rest of the disciples?

Read John 20:3-18.
How did the available disciples respond when they heard that Jesus' tomb was empty? (John 20:3-4)

What did they find? (John 20:5-9)

After the disciples left, Mary Magdalene stayed at the tomb for a while. In her grief and confusion, she looked into the tomb again. What did she see that hadn't been there before? (John 20:10-13)

Then what did she see? (John 20:14-16)

What was Mary instructed to do? (John 20:17-18)

Getting Personal—*How does Jesus' resurrection help you deal with the grief over someone you've buried?*

Read Matthew 28:2-15.
In case the disciples disputed Mary's word, the other women were able to back her up. What happened to them on their way back from the tomb? (Matthew 28:5-10)

But the women and the disciples weren't the only people concerned about the empty tomb and missing body. After the chief priests had gone to such trouble to make sure the tomb was guarded, they would be more than a little embarrassed if they couldn't produce Jesus' body. After all, the tomb was guarded by soldiers of the Roman Empire (perhaps the most capable and disciplined warriors in history). What did these Roman guards have to report to the chief priests? (Matthew 28:2-4)

What arrangement was made between the guards and religious leaders? (Matthew 28:11-15)

Getting Personal — *Knowing what you do about the character of the disciples, do you think you would have believed the story concocted by the Jewish religious leaders?*

Read Luke 24:13-43.
Jesus didn't appear only to the women after His resurrection. Two of His followers were walking from Jerusalem to Emmaus when the resurrected Jesus joined them (without allowing them to know who He was). These two followers provide a good idea of what the mood was during this turbulent time for Jesus' disciples. How did they feel? Why? (Luke 24:13-24)

What did Jesus do for these two? (Luke 24:25-32)

Even though these two witnesses had just walked the seven miles from Jerusalem to Emmaus, they returned "at once" to Jerusalem. They found Jesus' disciples there and compared what they knew. What exciting news did the "original" disciples have for the disciples from Emmaus? (Luke 24:33-35)

While they were all together talking, what happened? (Luke 24:36)

Everyone could hardly believe what he was seeing. What things did Jesus do to convince them that it was really He? (Luke 24:37-43)

Getting Personal — *Has Jesus' presence surprised you recently as it did the two men on the road?*

Read John 20:24-29.

One of Jesus' disciples (Thomas) was absent during Jesus' appearance to the group. And even though they all testified that Jesus had been there, Thomas refused to believe unless one certain thing came to pass. What did Thomas say he wanted before he would believe? (John 20:24-25)

How long did Thomas have to wait until he received what he asked for? (John 20:26)

What did Jesus say about belief? (John 20:27-29)

Getting Personal — *How does Jesus' statement about belief relate to you?*

Back to the Boats

Try to put yourself into the place of one of the disciples at this point. You've given up everything for the past three years or so to travel with Jesus and be "fishers of men." But to be truthful, Jesus had probably done most of the fishing. Now He is no longer with you, except for an occasional appearance here and there. What does your future hold? Is it time to make a career change? What happens if you decide to go home and Jesus appears while you're gone?

The disciples were probably still in a state of confusion. Even though they knew that Jesus was alive, their daily lives were certainly not the same as they had been prior to the Crucifixion. So one day Peter decided he was going fishing. Maybe he was trying to pass some time. Or perhaps he was thinking of returning to his original lifestyle. But since Peter had become somewhat of a leader, several of the other disciples decided to tag along.

Read John 21:1-23.
Based on their success, do you think they should have returned to fishing to earn a living? Explain (John 21:1-3).

How were they able to improve their "luck"? (John 21:4-6)

How did the disciples respond when they realized that their fishing advisor was really Jesus? (John 21:7-9)

Review Luke 5:1-11.
This passage describes one of the first encounters of Jesus with His disciples. What similarities do you recognize between this incident and the one in John 21?

The biblical account is very specific here, even to the point of letting us know exactly how many fish the disciples had netted (John 21:11). It is also specific in describing the mood of this meeting between Jesus and His disciples. It appears to be much more personal than His previous appearances. Jesus had singled out Thomas before. Here He selects Peter for a one-on-one conversation. But their discussion was a little repetitive. What was the basic content of their dialogue? (John 21:15-17)

Why do you think Jesus asked Peter the same question three times?

A Seed Is Planted

How did Jesus predict that Peter would die? Explain (John 21:18-19).

But Peter wasn't giving full attention to what Jesus wanted him to know. He interrupted and asked what was going to happen to John. How did Jesus answer him? (John 21:20-23)

Read Matthew 28:16-20.
What were some of Jesus' final instructions to His disciples?

Getting Personal — *Do you feel excited or guilty when you read Jesus' final instructions?*

Read Luke 24:44-53.
Where were the disciples to wait for further instructions? (Luke 24:44-49)

When was the last time Jesus was seen on earth? (Luke 24:50-51)

By the time Jesus finally left the disciples, how were they feeling? (Luke 24:52-53)

Read Mark 16:9-20.
These verses aren't found in the oldest (and most trustworthy) manuscripts from which this Gospel is translated. They were a later addition. That doesn't necessarily mean the verses are wrong, but this section has been misinterpreted by some people. Read it for yourself and see if you think that Jesus is saying that Christians should handle poisonous snakes and drink poison. If not, what do you think He is saying?

JOURNEY INWARD

As much as Jesus tried to prepare His followers for what would eventually happen to Him, they just weren't ready for His death and resurrection. Consequently, they went through some difficult times of doubt, fear, and confusion. The good news is that we can avoid those same negative emotions by learning from the mistakes of the disciples. So let's now consider the effects of **the reality of resurrection,** even for us today.

The essence of Christianity is in Jesus' resurrection. If Jesus hadn't risen from the dead, He still would have been a great person. But the Resurrection proves beyond a doubt all of Jesus' claims to be God. Consequently, a lot of people try to disprove the Resurrection in an attempt to undermine the Christian faith. But think about it.

❑ Do you really think Jesus' disciples could ever have summoned the courage to try to steal the body? And even if they did try, do you think they could have outmaneuvered a top-notch Roman guard? And even if they did outfox the Romans, do you think 10 of the 11 disciples would have been willing to die for what they knew to be a lie? (Tradition has it that all but John [and Judas, of course] were killed for their faith.) What do you think?

❑ If the Roman or Jewish officials had Jesus' body, why didn't they produce it as soon as everybody started talking about Jesus' resurrection? If they didn't want people to believe that Jesus rose from the dead, wouldn't they have shown the body right away? What do you think?

❑ If Jesus were really just a man faking death, do you think the guy could have endured the whippings, beatings, the spear in the side, the very real crucifixion, and being wrapped in 75 pounds of spices and cloth? Do you really think this person could have "woken up," rolled back a massive stone, frightened off a trained group of Roman guards, and then popped in and out of rooms to dazzle the people there? And if so, how was this guy able to do the miracles that Jesus had done prior to the Resurrection? What's your opinion?

The Resurrection makes sense. It's not just a myth to make Christians feel better. So spend a couple of minutes to consider what the Resurrection should mean to you.

❑ To Jesus, the Resurrection was the "payoff" to all His suffering and work on earth.

❑ To Peter, the Resurrection was the opportunity for a new relationship with the Master he had denied.

❑ To Joseph of Arimathea and Nicodemus, the Resurrection was proof that their faith in Jesus was not in vain.

❑ To the disciples on the road to Emmaus, Jesus' resurrection changed their perception of Him from God "undercover" to Messiah and Savior of the world.

❑ To all who observed it, the Resurrection was consolation that the raising of Lazarus was not just a one-shot conquest of death. If Jesus could do it for Lazarus, and if Jesus could do it for Himself, then surely He has the power to conquer death for all of us.

What does the Resurrection mean to you?

There are lots of answers to the above question. As you go about your regular activities, ask yourself that question every so often. No matter how down in the dumps you get (physically, emotionally, spiritually, etc.), the fact of the Resurrection always promises you another chance at recovery and triumph. Never give up on Jesus. He never gives up on you.

 KEY VERSE
"I am the Resurrection and the life. He who believes in Me will live, even though he dies; and whoever lives and believes in Me will never die. Do you believe this?" (John 11:25-26)

BEFORE YOU LEAVE

Before you toss this book on your shelf and forget about it, could we ask you to take a couple of minutes and fill out the survey on page 179? We value your input on our products as we try to target our materials for your specific needs. Please let us know what you think.

And if you thought this was an OK book, you may want to move on to Book 2 in the **BibleLog** series: *Good News To Go.* It begins where this book left off—the resurrection of Jesus—and shows what an effect that event had on the entire world. You can go through the book on your own, or a leader's guide is included if you want to get together with a small group to share and grow. Thanks for going this far through the **BibleLog** series.

GETTING TOGETHER

A Leader's Guide for Small Groups

Before you jump into this leader's guide in all the excitement of preparing for Session 1, take time to read these introductory pages.

Because the basic Bible content of the study is covered inductively in 12 chapters, group members should work through each assigned chapter before attending the small group meeting. This isn't always easy for busy adults, so encourage group members with a phone call or note between some of the meetings. Help them manage their time by pointing out how they can cover a few pages in a few minutes daily, and having them identify a regular time that they can devote to the **BibleLog** study.

Notice that each session is structured to include the following:

❑ Session Topic—a brief statement of purpose for the session.
❑ Icebreaker—an activity to help group members get better acquainted with the session topic and/or each other.
❑ Discussion Questions—a list of questions to encourage group participation.
❑ Optional Activities—supplemental ideas that will enhance your study.
❑ Assignment—directions for preparation and suggestions for memorization of key Scriptures.

Here are a few tips that can lead to more effective small group studies:

❑ Pray for each group member, asking the Lord to help you create an open atmosphere, so that everyone will feel free to share with each other and you.
❑ Encourage group members to bring their Bibles to each session. This series is based on the *New International Version*, but it is good to have several translations on hand for purposes of comparison.
❑ Start on time. This is especially important for the first meeting because it will set the pattern for the rest of the course.

❏ Begin with prayer, asking the Holy Spirit to open hearts and minds and to give understanding so that Truth will be applied.
❏ Involve everyone. As learners, we retain only 10 percent of what we hear, 20 percent of what we see, 65 percent of what we hear and see, *but* 90 percent of what we hear, see, and do.
❏ Promote a relaxed environment. Arrange your chairs in a circle or semi-circle. This promotes eye contact among members and encourages more dynamic discussion. Be relaxed in your own attitude and manner.

1

Session Topic: God wants us to evaluate our relationship with His Son, Jesus Christ.

Icebreakers *(choose one)*
1. Share your most unforgettable Christmas.
2. Describe the kinds of rituals or traditions you and your family observe at Christmas.

Discussion Questions
1. Has the Christmas story taken on real significance for you? Why or why not?
2. Do you think God has a plan for your life just as He did for Mary, Joseph, and the other people in the Christmas story?
3. How would you describe your relationship to God right now?
4. Has Jesus become the Word of God to you? (John 1:14) If so, when? Where have you allowed Jesus to make His "dwelling place" in your life?
5. Do you need to *begin, renew,* or *consider* a relationship with Jesus?

Prayer
Ask God to reveal Himself through His Word to you and others. Commit to carefully examining Jesus' life and ministry over the next 12 weeks to determine how you should respond to the Good News.

Optional Activities
1. Introduce this study with a film based on the life of Jesus, such as *Jesus of Nazareth* or *Jesus.* Invite the group over for a movie and popcorn, with discussion afterward.
2. Study Mary's Magnificat in Luke 1:46-55. List all the attributes of God found in Mary's praise song. Ask: **What can you learn from Mary's praise to improve your own praise life?**

Assignment
1. Complete Session 2.
2. Memorize John 1:14.

2

Session Topic: We can achieve our full potential only by adopting for ourselves the attitude Jesus displayed toward teamwork.

Icebreaker
Answer the following questions honestly:
1. Are you more like Loner Lenny or Welcoming Wilma when it comes to involving other people in your life?
2. Are you more like Tight-lipped Theo or Blabbermouth Belinda when it comes to calling attention to yourself or your positive attributes?
3. Are you more like Picky Paula or Friendly Freddy when it comes to including all types of people in your circle of friends?
4. Are you more like Griping Gary or Steadfast Stephanie when it comes to obeying Jesus when He asks you to do something?

Discussion Questions
1. Are we as a group trying to involve new people in our church? In our Sunday School classes? In our small group? Why or why not?
2. Are we as a group quick to point out our positive attributes to others?
3. Who are we excluding from this group? Why?

Prayer
Pray for faithfulness in working toward fulfilling your personal goals. Ask God to help you increase your capacity for teamwork.

Optional Activities
1. Do a character study of John the Baptist. Ask: **If John were here today, what would he eat and wear? Where would he preach repentance?**
2. Study the three temptations with which Satan tried to defeat Jesus. Discuss which of these temptations would have been the hardest to resist.

Assignment
1. Complete Session 3.
2. Memorize Matthew 4:19-20.

3

Session Topic: God wants us to live our lives according to the standards Jesus established in the Sermon on the Mount.

Icebreakers *(choose one)*
1. Make a list of popular advertising slogans and select the slogan that best represents your current philosophy of life. Discuss the values represented by each statement.
2. Complete the following statement: **When I compare my values and lifestyle with the values and lifestyle described by Jesus in His Sermon on the Mount, I feel . . .**

Discussion Questions
1. How would you rank yourself on each of the eight attitudes listed in the Beatitudes?
2. If you were to adopt Jesus' values as expressed in the Sermon on the Mount, what kind of changes would you expect to see in your life?
3. What risks would you be taking if you totally adopted Jesus' values for your lifestyle? What would make you willing to take those risks?

Prayer
Confide in God and a prayer partner any areas of your lifestyle that need work. Ask God to help each person develop a kingdom lifestyle.

Optional Activities
1. Identify the characteristics of Jesus' model prayer in Matthew 6:9-13. Ask: **How balanced is your prayer life?**
2. Lead the group in singing the song "Seek Ye First." Discuss how you can measure whether you are seeking first the kingdom of God.

Assignment
1. Complete Session 4.
2. Memorize Matthew 5:16. Think about some ways that others might realize that you as a Christian are different from people in the world.

4

Session Topic: God wants us to see each person we encounter as a potential friend for the good of His kingdom.

Icebreaker
Describe the relationship that Jesus had with: the Samaritan woman at the Well, the Adulterous Woman, Nicodemus the Pharisee, Zaccheus the Tax Collector, the Blind Man at Pool of Siloam, the Rich Young Man, Mary and Martha, the Pharisees.

Discussion Questions
1. How would you talk about spiritual things with a person you dislike?
2. What aspects of Jesus' conversation with each person or group in this session could you use as a model for discussions with your own friends, neighbors, and coworkers?
3. How are the following attitudes evident in Jesus model for building and improving relationships? What behaviors may result from these attitudes: equal acceptance of everyone, tolerance for silly questions, willingness to discuss spiritual things, initiation of conversations, lack of concern for personal advancement, vulnerability. On which of these do you need to work?

Prayer
Confess your weaknesses before God as well as your intentions for improving your relationships with others.

Optional Activities
1. Examine the "new birth" as taught in Jeremiah 31:31, 33; Ezekiel 11:19; 18:31; 36:26.
2. Keep a journal to see how God is working and helping you to improve your relationships with others.

Assignment
1. Complete Session 5.
2. Memorize John 3:16.

5

Session Topic: God wants us to allow His Son to work in our lives and help us reach our full potential.

Icebreakers *(choose one)*
1. Share any improvements you have made in problem relationships since the last session.
2. How do you respond to people who reject you?

Discussion Questions
1. How did Jesus show compassion through His miracles?
2. How did Jesus deal with each person's limitations?
3. What can we learn about Jesus' power from the miracles in this session?
4. What kind of potential did Jesus see in each person He healed?
5. Identify one limitation you have in each of the following areas: physique, emotions, and spirituality. Can any of these limitations prevent Jesus from helping you reach your full potential?

Prayer
Ask God to help you endure or overcome your limitations. Pray that the Holy Spirit will work in your life to eliminate attitudes that may be preventing you from reaching your full potential. Thank God for His compassion and guidance, both in the past and in the future.

Optional Activities
1. Reread Matthew 12:9-14. Describe your family's Sunday habits or traditions. Ask: **How does God intend us to spend the Sabbath or Sunday?**
2. Ask a physically disabled person to speak to the group. Ask him/her how God has helped him/her deal with the disability and reach his/her full potential.

Assignment
1. Complete Session 6.
2. Memorize Matthew 4:23. Identify the various aspects of Jesus' ministry in Galilee and how those same ministries are carried on today.

6

Session Topic: To fully appreciate Jesus' miracles, God wants us to get a new perspective on the "wonders" in our daily lives.

Icebreaker

Have you ever experienced or witnessed what you consider to be a "miracle"?

Discussion Questions

1. Do you ever refuse to recognize God's power in your life? Give some examples of times when you've rationalized or explained away God's "little wonders" in your life.
2. How can you be more aware of God's work in your daily life?
3. What proof of God's power can you see in nature? Your family? Your work? Your church?

Prayer

Give thanks for God's "little wonders" that surround you. Thank God for answered prayer.

Optional Activities

1. Ask a doctor or surgeon to describe for your group some of the "wondrous" functions of the human body.
2. Ask a group member to read and report on *Fearfully and Wonderfully Made* by Dr. Paul Brand and Philip Yancey (Zondervan), a study of the human body.
3. Spend some time hiking. Try to photograph some interesting scenes of nature. What was the most "wondrous" thing you saw during your hike? Develop a slide show or photo display based on the miracles of nature.

Assignment

1. Complete Session 7.
2. Memorize John 14:12-14. Note that we are to bring everything to Jesus in prayer and to have confidence that He will answer our prayers.

7

Session Topic: God wants us to use our minds to think about and understand our faith.

Icebreakers *(choose one)*
1. Complete the following sentence: **During the past week, the most remarkable thing in my life that could qualify as a "wonder" is . . .**
2. Describe your favorite parable in today's language with more recent illustrations.

Discussion Questions
1. If Jesus really wanted His followers to understand truth, why did He tell parables that sometimes seemed obscure?
2. How did Jesus help the disciples apply His parables?
3. Review the parables on relationships studied during this session. What applications can you find for your relationships today based on the principles Jesus expressed in this session's parables?
4. Read the modern-day parable, "The Land of Halfway." What did the man understand? What can you tell about the man's church habits? How does this parable apply to you? Do you ever do anything halfway?

Prayer
Thank God for giving us minds to think about and apply His principles in our lives.

Optional Activities
1. Discuss the importance of having a quiet or devotional time with God on a regular basis. Set aside a few minutes each day to clearly focus your thoughts on God and His Word.
2. Review the key verses for Sessions 1–6.

Assignment
1. Complete Session 8.
2. Memorize Matthew 13:34-35. Read Psalm 78 and examine the prophecy that relates to these key verses.

THE LAND OF HALFWAY

(A Parable)

Once upon a time a man from our world was transferred by his company to the Land of Halfway. The Land of Halfway is just like ours, except for one small difference–the people there only do things halfway.

All their books are missing the second half—but it doesn't matter since no one finishes anything he begins reading. The roads are dangerous because cars lack half their parts—and drivers never completely learn to control their vehicles. Houses don't have roofs; bridges go exactly halfway across rivers; gloves, shoes, and socks are sold in single units instead of pairs. Even Baskin-Robbins ice cream stores offer only 15 1/2 flavors.

As you might imagine, the man who was transferred to the Land of Halfway had a terrible time trying to adjust to the odd customs and habits. Just getting from one place to another was a challenge. He would stop to "half fill 'er up" at a gas station and ask directions—only to be told how to get halfway to where he needed to go. Meals never got around to dessert, and his hair looked terrible after he went to the barber shop and got half a haircut.

After a frustrating week of living in the Land of Halfway, the man was ready to take his own life—but was afraid he wouldn't go all the way through with it. He couldn't adjust at work because every time he got halfway through a project, his supervisor gave him a new assignment. Every time a song on the radio was halfway through, the disc jockey would begin another one. And he especially hated reading the newspaper, seeing "continued on page 57," and discovering that page 57 didn't exist.

The newspaper did contain an ad for a nearby church, however, so he decided to give it a try. The sanctuary was half full, of course. Yet the sermon was quite good. And to the man's surprise, it was complete!

Later, as the people filed out of the church, the man asked one of the members, "Why didn't the preacher just preach half a sermon? This is the first time I've seen anything completed in the Land of Halfway."

"Don't you know?" the church member replied. "A sermon's not complete unless somebody responds to it. We all just go home now and forget about what we've heard."

The man understood. And for the first time in a week, he felt right at home.

8

Session Topic: God provides us with resources that can help us understand His mysteries more completely.

Icebreakers *(choose one)*
1. Describe the best mystery you ever read.
2. Find a copy of a "5-minute" mystery book and solve one of the mysteries.

Discussion Questions
1. What are some questions about God, Jesus, religion, or the Bible that seem unanswerable to you?
2. In what ways are Jesus' parables concerning relationships (Session 7) similar to His parables about the kingdom of God (Session 8)?
3. Are there any similarities between the kingdom parables?
4. Read Matthew 13:9 and discuss how Jesus' challenge in this verse explains the key verse for this session. How does faith improve our spiritual insight?

Prayer
Ask God to help you continue pursuing answers to your questions so you can encourage others.

Optional Activities
1. Create a skit illustrating the main principle of one or more of the following kingdom parables: Growing Seed (Mark 4:26-29); Mustard Seed (Matthew 13:31-32); Yeast (Matthew 13:33); Hidden Treasure (Matthew 13:44); Pearl (Matthew 13:45-46); New (Matthew 13:47-50).
2. Research the resources available to you such as Bible commentaries, Bible dictionaries, study Bibles, Bible concordances, and word studies. Summarize the tools on a notecard for future reference.

Assignment
1. Complete Session 9.
2. Memorize Matthew 13:11-12. Remember that God has promised to make His secrets known to us as indicted in these key verses.

9

Session Topic: God wants us to develop spiritual habits and discipline.

Icebreakers (*choose one*)
1. Complete the following statements with as many excuses as possible:
   - ❏ I didn't workout or exercise today because . . .
   - ❏ I didn't do my work today because . . .
   - ❏ I didn't spend time with God or His Word today because . . .
2. Share any new aspects of Jesus' character that you discovered in your study of His teachings.

Discussion Questions
1. What are some ways we learn to discipline ourselves physically to exercise or workout?
2. How do we maintain good work habits?
3. Can any of these types of discipline be used in our spiritual lives?
4. What are some ways to overcome laziness? Overcommitment to our social lives? Discouragement due to our failures?
5. What are some ways we can help each other develop spiritual habits?

Prayer
Ask God to help you devote more time to developing spiritual discipline.

Optional Activities
1. Invite an athlete to speak to your group about the importance of exercise and training in his or her sport. Compare the preparation that goes into physical fitness with that of spiritual fitness.
2. Read Matthew 10:37-39 and share how Christ's teachings have united or divided the members of your family.

Assignment
1. Complete Session 10.
2. Memorize Matthew 10:37-39.

10

Session Topic: God wants us to follow Jesus' example when we face rejection.

Icebreakers *(choose one)*
1. List as many reasons as possible that you or your friends reject other people. Supplement the group's list with the following: physical appearance, including skin color, weight, and disabilities; mental and physical ability; political, sexual, and religious preferences; economic status.
2. With whom do you find it hardest to be accepted as a person of worth and special value? Strangers? Family members? Best friend? Church members? Spouse?

Discussion Questions
1. List some examples of rejection faced by Jesus.
2. How did Jesus deal with each form of rejection?
3. Which of the following best describes how you deal with feelings of rejection: indifference, moping, tears, bitterness, laughter, openness?
4. What are some Scriptures that have helped you when you faced rejection? Brainstorm some ways to handle rejection.
5. What positive results might come from rejection?

Prayer
Silently commit yourself to following Jesus' example when faced with rejection.

Optional Activities
1. Obtain several maps of Jerusalem and the surrounding areas. Trace Jesus' path during the last week before His crucifixion.
2. Review John 15:18-19. Ask: **What troubles and pressures may we experience as we live Christian lives in the world?**

Assignment
1. Complete Session 11.
2. Memorize John 15:18-19.

11

Session Topic: God wants us to model sacrificial love to others.

Icebreakers *(choose one)*
1. List as many expressions or kinds of love as possible.
2. Complete the sentence: **I love . . .**

Discussion Questions
1. Share a time when you have experienced agape or self-sacrificing love.
2. Where does agape love ultimately come from?
3. How does Jesus express agape love to us?
4. Complete the following statement : **I can show agape love to the other people in this group by. . . .**
5. List some specific actions that communicate agape love.

Prayer
Thank Jesus for His sacrificial love. Praise God for His grace.

Optional Activities
1. Discuss the three different Greek words for love: *eros* (physical or sexual attraction that is triggered by emotion); *phileo* (tender affection based on mutual attraction or brotherly love); *agape* (self-sacrificial love that does not seek anything in return). Explain that *agape* is the word for love that is used most often in the Bible.
2. Do a comparison study of the Passover (Exodus 12–13) and Jesus' celebration of Passover (Matthew 26:17-30; Mark 14:12-26; Luke 22:7-39; John 13:1-30).
3. Study your church's views and doctrines relating to the Lord's Supper. Ask your pastor or a church officer to meet with your group and share the significance of this ordinance in your church.

Assignment
1. Complete Session 12.
2. Memorize Mark 15:37-39.

12

Session Topic: God wants us to understand the impact of Jesus' resurrection for us today.

Icebreaker
Spend some time thinking about death and funerals. Ask: **What is the hardest funeral you've ever had to attend?**

Discussion Questions
1. List as many ways as possible that people attempt to disprove the resurrection of Jesus Christ.
2. What kind of evidence can you compile to defend the Resurrection?
3. What conclusion can be drawn from all evidence?
4. How can you worship God for the impact of Jesus' resurrection on your life? What does Jesus' resurrection mean to you?

Prayer
Praise God for raising His Son from the dead.

Optional Activities
1. Discuss Thomas' doubts about Jesus' resurrection. Ask: **If you could ask God one thing to improve your faith, what would it be? Do you ever experience spiritual doubts? What have you found helpful at these times?**
2. Have your group express what Jesus' resurrection means to them by writing a haiku. A haiku is a Japanese poem that has three unrhymed lines with 5 syllables, 7 syllables, and 5 syllables. For example:

Resurrection means (5)
new life for me and for you (7)
for eternity. (5)

Assignment
1. Review sessions 1–12.
2. Memorize John 11:25-26.

REVIEW

Session Topic: God wants us to remember and apply what we've learned about Him in the Gospels. Choose one or two review methods, based on the size and interests of your group.

Option 1

Play "Stump the Panel." Ask several volunteers to participate on two panels. The remainder of the group should write questions about the Gospels, trying to stump the panels with their questions. If one panel is unable to answer a question, the question is passed to their opponents. Keep score to make this competitive.

Option 2

Use the names and places found in each chapter to play "Wheel of Fortune" or "Probe" with your group. New group members or members who missed several sessions will be able to participate since they merely have to choose consonants to fill in the blanks on a chalkboard or poster board. Be sure to alert each team whether the words are people, places, things, or phrases.

Option 3

Review by providing group members with the opportunity to raise questions, discuss problems, or share opinions on issues that had to be omitted during the course.

Option 4

Review the key verses from each session. Provide some sort of reward or certificate for all group members who have memorized all key verses.

Option 5

Ask: How has this study affected your relationship with Jesus Christ? Have you begun, renewed, or considered the possibility of a relationship with Jesus Christ?

WRAP-UP

BibleLog Book 1

Please take a minute to fill out and mail this form giving us your candid reaction to this material. Thanks for your help!

1. In what setting did you use this **BibleLog** study?

If you used Book 1 for personal study only, skip to question 6.
2. How many people were in your group?

3. What was the age-range of those in your group?

4. How many weeks did you spend on this study?

5. How long was your average meeting time?

6. Did you complete the studies before discussing them with a group?

7. How long did it take you to complete the study on your own?

8. Do you plan to continue the **BibleLog** Series? Why or why not?

Would you like more information on Bible study resources for small groups?

Name _____

Address _____

Church _____

City _____ State _____ Zip _____

```
PLACE
STAMP
HERE
```

Adult Education Editor
Victor Books
1825 College Avenue
Wheaton, Illinois 60187